She Talks Magazine

FEATURING

Rushia Brown

Celebrating
WOMEN'S
HISTORY MONTH

WWW.SHETALKSMAG.COM

She Talks Magazine Vol. 1 Issue 3
March 2024

Cover Image
Joshua Ducharme

Design/Layout
JD Consulting Solutions

Editorial
Julie Ducharme Editor in Chief
Tia Cristy Lifestyle Editor
Shelby Jo Long Business Editor
Luba Sakharuk Women in Tech Editor

Contributors
Belinda Jane
Kim Adele Randal
Lisa E. Kirkwood
Ada Hsieh
Eve Nasby
Tia Cristy
Julie Ducharme
Luba Sakharuk
Andrea Bell
Shelby Jo Long
Daniela Santangelo
Nuirka Castaneda
Terrilani Chong
Wendy Watson
Shannon Missimer
Heather Coe Clark

If you are interested in writing a column or advertising please visit shetalksmag.com

Copyright © 2024. All Rights Reserved.

She Talks Magazine

Table of CONTENTS

5   **REDEFINING LEGACY**
The Evolution of Modern Matriarchy

8   **THE HEART OF A LION**

11   **HISTORICAL PORTRAITS OF BRAVERY**
Courageous Women who Defied Old Rules, Redefined Empowerment, and Built Legacies

17   **A BRIEF HISTORY OF LIPSTICK**
How a Beauty Product Became a Symbol of Rebellion

21   **FASHION VISIONARIES**
Shaping Style and Sustainability

26   **A JOURNEY OF FAITH & ENDURANCE: THE REMARKABLE SAGA OF ALICE WALSH STRONG**

SHETALKS MAGAZINE

FEATURED ARTICLE

 **RUSHA BROWN: GROWNING UP WNBA**

A LEAGUE OF THEIR OWN

 **NAVIGATING EMPOWERMENT**

TIPS FROM TIA

 **TRANSCENDING BARRIERS**

THE INCREDIBLE FEMALE CEO

 **FLORENCE HALL**

A Pioneer in the Medical Field

FROM FORT LIVING ROOM TO FORT KNOX: BEATRICE'S JOURNEY OF ADVERSITY AND TRIUMPH

EMPOWERING WOMEN LEADERS: KEY INSIGHTS FOR OPTIMIZING SUCCESS

Key Insights for Optimizing Success

CULTIVATING GRATITUDE IN CHALLENGING TIMES: A GUIDE FOR RESILIENCE

#I AM THE VETERAN

REDEFINING LEGACY

The Evolution of Modern Matriarchy

BY DANIELA SANTANGELO

Women's History Month is not just a celebration of the women who came before us; it's a time to reflect on the legacy we are creating for future generations. For me, this reflection has become especially poignant after the loss of my grandfather on Christmas – a man who embodied kindness, generosity, and the secure patriarchy of his time. With his passing, our family dynamics shifted, placing the spotlight on the strong matriarchal figure at our dinner table – my great-grandmother, an immigrant who arrived in the United States from Italy with only $3 in her pocket.

As I navigate the complexities of modern life, the intersection of immigration and entrepreneurship weighs heavily on my mind. I feel a profound responsibility to carry on the legacy of my ancestors, but with a twist. I am compelled to forge a path that is not just financially successful but also sustainable, purpose-driven, and focused on well-being.

My journey has not been without its struggles. For much of my life, I battled with co-dependency, an often anxious and depressive struggle that left a significant impact on my self-worth.

As I embarked on my first entrepreneurial journey in 2016 co-founding a company I endured key moments that would shape my ancestral lineage.

Here I was as a new mom and startup executive, I found myself In the depths of postpartum depression, standing in front of a mirror, seeing a reflection of a woman who felt stuck and unsure of how to break free.

I was entangled in a business and relationship that had left me feeling powerless. Yet, within the complexity of that struggle, I found a way out when my husband left, leaving me with our two young boys. In that departure, I discovered an unexpected strength – the strength to reclaim my life.

As a single mother, my focus shifted from the constraints of a toxic relationship to the empowerment that came with raising two boys. Motherhood became a catalyst for change, propelling me to reevaluate my priorities and rediscover my own strength. Through the challenges, I learned that nurturing self-confidence in young girls is not only vital for their personal growth but also instrumental in shaping the trajectory of their lives.

In my pursuit of this vision, I sacrificed a great deal to build my startup. However, life took an unexpected turn when I faced a high-conflict divorce and found myself pushed out of my own creation. Instead of viewing this as a setback, I saw it as a calling – an opportunity to rewrite history in a way that diverges from the traditional roles my matriarchal ancestors embraced.

It started with a rediscovery of self. A friend shared a quote with me,

> "REMEMBER THAT LIFE'S GREATEST LESSONS ARE USUALLY LEARNED AT THE WORSE TIMES AND FROM THE WORST MISTAKES."

I quickly realized the foundational pillars I needed to establish during this time of starting over. I distilled it down to 3 aspects:
1. Your Narrative
2. Your Network
3. Your Mindset

A LEGACY THAT TRANSENDS

In the face of adversity, I realized that the decisions I make today will shape the future lineage of my family. No longer confined to the role of a homemaker, I am determined to create a legacy that extends beyond societal expectations. It is a legacy built on resilience, innovation, and a commitment to making a positive impact on the world. I started to shape my narrative from a place of strength and not victimization. I started to visualize my future state and embody it now.

Suddenly, aligned introductions to people started appearing in my life. Network and community building has been a strength of mine that I contribute entirely to my grandparents. After my grandfather started his construction company, his home became known as an "incubator" for others immigrating over trying to find their way into a job and a community. That give back mentality has allowed me to mentor companies at Techstars Miami and continue on to advise startups on how to navigate the pitfalls of the entrepreneurial journey from a business & a wellness perspective. At the end of the day, your mindset becomes the most powerful asset to realizing your dreams and unlimited possibilities that await. It requires practice. A lot of practice. I embarked on a 9 month journey to obtain my meditation teaching certification and positive psychology coach. This experience provided me an opportunity to learn self-healing modalities and frameworks that I can teach to others.

After co-founding a company that raised $30m and having to divorce the CEO, I lost my soul in the process and aim to ensure others can avoid this devastating experience.

As I rebuild, I am intentional about infusing sustainability and purpose into every aspect of my life and work. My grandparents immigration journey of starting anew with only a few dollars in their pocket inspires me to overcome challenges with a tenacious spirit. I want my legacy to reflect not just financial success but a commitment to leaving the world a better place for future generations.

Women's History Month is a reminder that our stories are still being written. As a modern matriarch, I am proud to carry the torch of my ancestors, but I am equally excited to illuminate a new path. By challenging stereotypes, embracing change, and focusing on sustainability and purpose, I am contributing to a legacy that transcends time – one that will shape the narrative of women's history for generations to come.

The Heart of a Lion

BY EVE NASBY

"In order to know the strength of the anchor, we need to feel the strength of the storm."

— CORRIE TEN BOOM

Entrepreneurship is not for the faint of heart or for those who lack courage. There are highs and lows, adversity and wins which seem to balance each other like two kids on a teeter totter. But how much is too much when it comes to obstacles and challenges? When do you just throw up your hands and surrender to the fact that the sumo wrestler on the other end of the teeter totter is just not going to get off?

Corrie ten Boom endured unimaginable hardship and trauma during World War II. Yet she emerged with an awe-inspiring ability to forgive, advocate for hope and reconciliation,

By Unknown photographer - De geschiedenis van de familie Ten Boom (1921), Public Domain, https://commons.wikimedia.org/w/index.php?curid=58051064

> "Worry does not empty tomorrow of its sorrow. It empties today of its strength."

and inspire resilience in others after enduring numerous trials. Her life story provides striking lessons for us as entrepreneurs regarding the incredible human capacity for resilience.

Born in Haarlem, Netherlands in 1892, ten Boom lived a comfortable, contented life as a middle-aged watchmaker focused on the craft passed down from generations before her and sharing her faith enthusiastically with others.

In 1922, she became the first licensed female watchmaker in Holland. When the Nazis invaded, ten Boom and her family provided shelter for 800 Jews, becoming part of the underground resistance movement during intense persecution. They soon faced harsh consequences when the family was arrested on February 28, 1944 for concealing persons being sought by the Nazis.

Ten Boom's suffering had only just begun. Her father died 10 days after arrest at age 84 and her sister Nollie endured unspeakable cruelty before perishing in Ravensbrück concentration camp. Corrie and her

US Holocaust Memorial Museum

sister Betsie were transferred through camps before Betsie also died in December 1944. Alone, frightened but fortified by an inner resilience and conviction, ten Boom persevered imprisonment until her miraculous release on December 28, 1944 due to a clerical error.

> "The measure of a life, after all, is not its duration, but its donation."

At age 84, ten Boom had traveled over 60 countries telling her tale over 50 years. Though wheelchair bound in those latter decades, she never lost her fighting spirit, modeling for the world the very

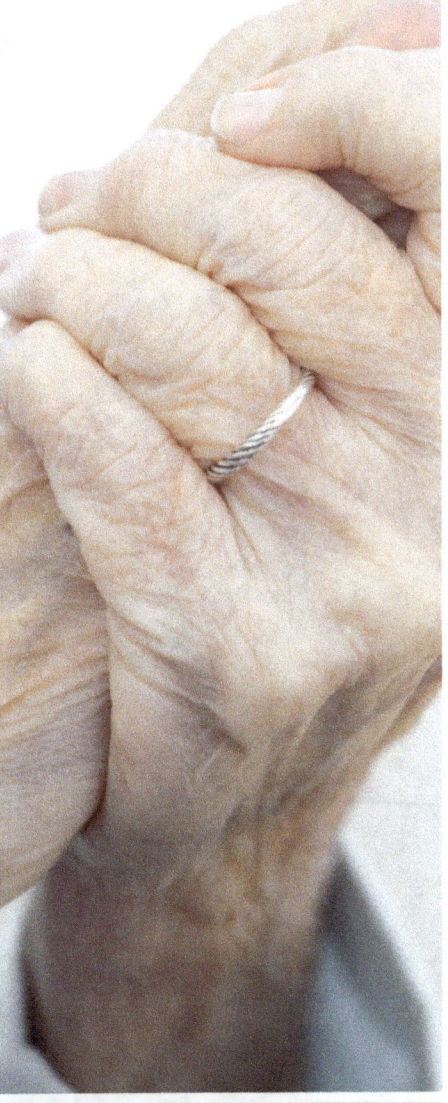

Most entrepreneurs have not suffered such extreme personal calamity, but perhaps you have weathered your own storms - a betrayal, lawsuit, bankruptcy, losing a business. Ten Boom's story offers lessons on anchoring our inner resilience no matter what the storm and rising like a phoenix out of the ashes.

Starting over at age 52 after burying her entire family, ten Boom courageously turned hardship into redemption. Her writing and global speaking engagements shared tales of hope, and resilience through faith and how love can overcome any evil. Ten Boom reminded that victim and perpetrator alike remained human, no

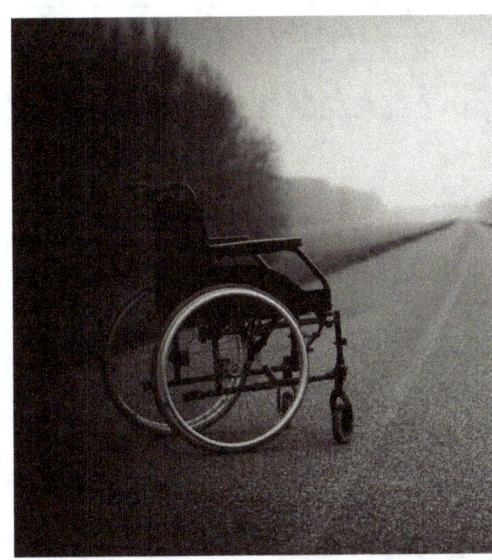

meaning of perseverance through adversity. Ten Boom's legacy remains the incredible example of her courageous resilience even

matter how persecution warped one's humanity. By sharing her story, ten Boom exemplified moving beyond bitterness into grace, evidencing the promise of renewal.

at the darkest times, reminding us no matter the trauma - with faith, fellowship and defiance of spirit - better days will come.

UPCOMING She Talks

Coronado, CA

Women's Product Entrepreneur & Inventor Summit

April 27-28 2024

Gilbert, AZ

Women in Aviation

May 18 2024

Coronado, CA

Great Gatsby Gala

May 18 2024

BOOK NOW

leadandempowerher.com

HISTORICAL PORTRAITS OF BRAVERY

Courageous Women who Defied Old Rules, Redefined Empowerment, and Built Legacies

by Lisa E. Kirkwood

March 8th is International Women's Day, and March of each year is Women's History Month - a time to celebrate women's contributions to history, culture, and society.

In honor of the extraordinary women pioneers from the past who paved the way for future generations, I dedicate this feature to them. Thank you for improving and transforming lives for all of us!

This brief history lesson mentions in chronological order only a few of my personal favorites, role models, and trailblazing women whom I personally admire and who can inspire anyone, women and men alike, in many ways.

Here are some highlights of their lifelong achievements and the lasting legacies they built.

"The future belongs to those who believe in the beauty of their dreams."

- Eleanor Roosevelt
former first lady of the United States

ELIZABETH I

Queen of England
(1533 –1603)

One of the world's longest reigning monarchs a few centuries ago, she came to power in a male-dominated and ruled society, during a dark era when wars were raging on all continents.

During her decades-long reign, England became a global colonial power, culture and arts flourished, and Shakespearean theater was created.

The queen had countless achievements, and two movie adaptations were made starring Kate Blanchett in the title role. The movies depicting her life shed some light on the historical facts and the complex relationships between social strata at that time.

Despite criticism, excess, and controversy associated with colonialism, Queen Elizabeth I left a lasting and influential legacy, and the English language spread across the world being now the main language of communication between people of various nationalities.

By Unknown author - This file was derived from: Elizabeth I in coronation robes.jpg:, Public Domain, https://commons.wikimedia.org/w/index.php?curid=80213975

MARIE CURIE
(1867 –1934)

A Polish and naturalized-French physicist and chemist who conducted pioneering research on radioactivity.

Since she was awarded the prestigious Nobel prize together with her husband, some people pointed out that she was just a contributor to her husband's work, without giving her proper credit. Nonetheless, she was the first woman to win a Nobel Prize, the first person to win a Nobel Prize twice, and the only person to win a Nobel Prize in two scientific fields.

Marie Curie was also recognized for her huge contribution to finding treatments for cancer, and, in 1906, she was the first woman to become a professor at the University of Paris. She also received many honorary degrees from universities across the world.

In addition to helping to overturn established ideas in physics and chemistry, Marie Curie's work has had a profound effect in society, where she had to overcome gender barriers to attain her scientific achievements. She has also become an icon in pop culture.

By Henri Manuel - cdn-images-1.medium.com, Public Domain, https://commons.wikimedia.org/w/index.php?curid=61396200

Amelia Earhart
An American aviation pioneer

By Underwood (active 1880 – c. 1950)[1] - http://amextbg2.wgbhdigital.org/wgbh/americanexperience/media/uploads/special_features/photo_gallery/amelia_gallery_07.jpg, Public Domain, https://commons.wikimedia.org/w/index.php?curid=57938262

An American aviation pioneer and writer, born in 1897, she was the first female aviator to fly solo across the Atlantic Ocean, promoting aviation and competitive flying.

Although Earhart had gained fame for her transatlantic flight, her ideas on marriage were liberal for that time, as she believed in equal responsibilities for both breadwinners and proudly kept her own maiden's name after marriage.

Earhart's accomplishments in aviation inspired a generation of female aviators, including the more than 1,000 women pilots of the Women Airforce Service Pilots (WASP) who ferried military aircraft, towed gliders, flew target practice aircraft, and served as transport pilots during World War II.

Amelia Earhart was a successful and heavily promoted writer who served as aviation editor for Cosmopolitan magazine from 1928 to 1930. She wrote magazine articles, newspaper columns, and essays, and published two books based upon her experiences as a flyer during her lifetime.

The home where Earhart was born is now the Amelia Earhart Birthplace Museum and is maintained by The Ninety-Nines, an international group of female pilots of whom Earhart was the first elected president.

By Harris & Ewing - This image is available from the United States Library of Congress#039;s Prints and Photographs division under the digital ID hec.40747.This tag does not indicate the copyright status of the attached work. A normal copyright tag is still required. See Commons: Licensing., Public Domain, https://commons.wikimedia.org/w/index.php?curid=25878426

Her last flight and subsequent disappearance in 1937 at a relatively young age drove her to lasting fame in global culture. Hundreds of articles and scores of books have been written about her life, which is often cited as a motivational tale, especially for girls. Earhart is generally regarded as a feminist icon known in her lifetime and beyond for her charismatic appeal, independence, persistence, coolness under pressure, courage, and goal-oriented career.

By Originally uploaded by w:User:Logawi - Transferred from en.wikipedia, description page is/was here., Public Domain, https://commons.wikimedia.org/w/index.php?curid=1308910

PEARL S. BUCK *1892-1973*

SHE Talks Mag *Historical Portraits of Bravery*

By Agip - [1] Dutch National Archives, The Hague, Fotocollectie Algemeen Nederlands Persbureau (ANEFO), 1945-1989 Bestanddeelnummer 925-7294, CC BY-SA 3.0 nl, https://commons.wikimedia.org/w/index.php?curid=20465084

American novelist, winner of the Nobel prize for literature and numerous other literary awards. She wrote memoirs, short stories, children's books, and highly acclaimed novels translated in many languages throughout the world.

Pearl S. Buck is best known for *The Good Earth*, the best-selling novel in the United States in 1931 and 1932, and which won her the Pulitzer Prize in 1932. In 1938, she became the first American woman to win the Nobel Prize in Literature "for her rich and truly epic descriptions of peasant life in China" and for her "masterpieces", two memoir-biographies of her missionary parents.

A highly educated woman and a prolific writer, she spent most of her life in China, depicting endearing characters in poetic and realistic manner at the same time.

Pearl S. Buck was committed to a range of issues that were largely ignored by her generation. She wrote on diverse subjects, including women's rights, Asian cultures, immigration, adoption, missionary work, war, the atomic bomb, and violence.

Long before it was considered fashionable or politically safe to do so, Buck challenged the American public by raising consciousness on topics such as racism, sex discrimination, and the plight of Asian war children.

In 1949, after finding that existing adoption services considered Asian and mixed-race children unadoptable, Buck founded the first permanent foster home for US-born mixed-race children of Asian descent, which she named *The Welcome Home*.

Buck combined the careers of wife, mother, author, editor, international spokesperson, and political activist, and she became well-known as an advocate for civil rights, women's rights, disability rights, and humanitarian works.

American writer Pearl Buck at her desk in Philadelphia in 1968. (AP) https://www.theatlantic.com/international/archive/2012/08/what-the-remarkable-legacy-of-pearl-buck-still-means-for-china/260918/

"People always say that I didn't give up my seat because I was tired, but that isn't true. I was not tired physically ... No, the only tired I was, was tired of giving in."

- Rosa Parks

By Unknown author - USIA / National Archives and Records Administration Records of the U.S. Information Agency Record Group 306, Public Domain, https://commons.wikimedia.org/w/index.php?curid=4344206

By Gene Herrick for the Associated Press; restored by Adam Cuerden - http://www.rmyauctions.com/lot-8002.aspx, Public Domain, https://commons.wikimedia.org/w/index.php?curid=81795628

Rosa Parks
(1913 –2005)

A prominent activist and civil rights leader, she became a pivotal symbol in America's Civil Rights Movement after she refused to move to the back of a city bus in Montgomery, Alabama, in 1955, at a time when color segregation between white and black was enforced and considered legal.

Following her arrest and then release, she triggered a massive social movement that not only abolished racial segregation on public transportation in the American South but paved the way for racial equality throughout the USA and the world.

Overcoming adversities, gender and race stereotypes, Rosa Parks received numerous awards for her civic activism, and became an icon of popular culture, film, and television. The United States Congress has honored her as "the first lady of civil rights" and "the mother of the freedom movement".

MOTHER THERESA
(1910 – 1997)

SHE Talks Mag *Historical Portraits of Bravery*

She was an Albanian-Indian Catholic nun and the founder of the Missionaries of Charity. Transcending religious denominations and focusing on people, regardless of their confessions of faith, in 1979, Mother Teresa received the Nobel Peace Prize "for work undertaken in the struggle to overcome poverty and distress, which also constitutes a threat to peace".

She donated her Nobel prize money to the poor people in India. When Mother Teresa received the prestigious prize, she was asked, "What can we do to promote world peace?" She answered, "Go home and love your family."

At the time of her death, the Missionaries of Charity had numerous branches worldwide operating clinics and community homes, offering counseling programs for the underprivileged, supporting orphanages and schools.

Portrayed in documentaries and books, films, and television, Mother Teresa has been commemorated by museums and named the patroness of a number of churches. She has had

By Kingkong photo; www.celebrity-photos.com from Laurel Maryland, USA - Mother Teresa best © copyright 2010, CC BY-SA 2.0, https://commons.wikimedia.org/w/index.php?curid=74493804

buildings, roads, and complexes named after her.

She was honored by governments and civilian organizations and appointed an honorary Companion of the Order of Australia in 1982 "for service to the community of Australia and humanity at large".

Some of these brave women, and many others like them, may have chosen different paths, but their life purpose and enduring missions share many commonalities. Such amazing ladies continue to influence and inspire us for generations to come.

With more or most women in power, we would all enjoy a less troubled history, and a much brighter future, where humanity prevails, and people can live in peace and harmony. Let's do this together!

By Series: Reagan White House Photographs, 1/20/1981 - 1/20/1989 Collection: White House Photographic Collection, 1/20/1981 - 1/20/1989 - Public Domain, https://commons.wikimedia.org/w/index.php?curid=94635435

References: Google, Wikipedia. Article by Lisa E. Kirkwood – The True Stories Merchant
www.thetruestoriesmerchant.com

A BRIEF HISTORY OF

LIPSTICK

HOW A BEAUTY PRODUCT BECAME A SYMBOL OF REBELLION

By Ada Hsieh

Since the 19th century, lipstick has been a popular cosmetic item used to enhance beauty and femininity. But during the suffragette days, lipstick took on a different role; it became a sign of rebellion. As women around the world fought for their right to vote, lipstick was seen as a symbol of the feminist movement. Let's take a brief look at the history of lipstick and how it came to represent a powerful statement of female empowerment.

Lipstick has been around for thousands of years, with the first signs of it being used by ancient civilizations. Egyptians are credited with the invention of lipstick, using a mix of crushed bugs and henna to color their lips. Ancient Sumerians also used lip rouge made from gemstones and crushed plants to create a reddish-tinted pigment.

During the middle ages in Europe, lip coloring was used by both men and women, but the higher class often shamed the lower class for wearing makeup.

During the Victorian era, makeup was seen as vulgar and any woman who wore it was labeled as promiscuous. Lipstick was still popular, but it wasn't until the 20th century that it began to be seen as a sign of power and rebellion. It started during the suffragette movement in Britain, when women started wearing red lipstick as a show of strength and solidarity. The trend quickly spread to other countries and lipstick came to be associated with feminism and female empowerment.

BEAUTY, TO ME, IS BEING COMFORTABLE IN YOUR OWN SKIN.

— GWYNETH PALTROW

Red lipstick was popularized during the early 20th century, but before then it was associated with morally dubious women such as actresses, courtesans, and prostitutes.

Legend has it - the use of red lipstick as a symbol of resistance dates back to 1912 in the United States, when suffragette leaders Elizabeth Cady Stanton and Charlotte Perkins Gilman marched wearing the vibrant shade to gain more attention to their cause because of its ability to shock men. Historians say this is likely a concocted story released by the famous cosmetics company, Arden. As the story goes, red lipstick became a symbol of strength and assertiveness, and cosmetic stores even handed out tubes of bright red lipstick to the marching women. Later, British suffragette leader Emmeline Pankhurst donned the same red lip to stand in solidarity with her American sisters. This is the first use of lipstick as a way to make a statement against the status quo and fight for women's rights. It may just have been a marketing scheme, but the reality of it is that the impact of using lipstick as a sign of rebellion quickly grew in popularity among suffragettes and spread worldwide. While the movement was originally centered around fighting for the right of women to vote, it soon evolved into a broader symbol of empowerment for anyone looking to make a statement. This message of strength, resilience and determination was taken up by feminist groups in the 1960s, who popularized the use of bright lipstick colors as a form of non-violent protest.

It didn't stop there either. "The How" it started may have been made up, but "The Why" is rooted in tangible human and civil rights history. Here are more examples of using red lipstick as defiance and resilience in recent history that are true.

In Nicaragua in 2018, Nicaraguan men and women sported red lipstick and uploaded photos of themselves to social media to show their support for their political movement. Similarly, in Chile in 2019, almost 10,000 women took to the streets with black blindfolds and red lips to denounce sexual violence. More recently, in Portugal in 2021, Portuguese politicians and citizens took to social media posting images of themselves wearing a bright red lip after presidential candidate Andre Ventura insulted MP Marisa Matias for her red lips.

During World War II, wearing red lipstick became a sign of patriotism and a statement against facism. It seemed Hitler also detested the color of red lipstick. Women were told to paint their lips with a patriotic and morale-boosting colour. When lipstick taxes made wearing lipstick prohibitively expensive in the UK, women stained their lips with beet juice instead. All of this shows that the use of red lipstick as a symbol of resistance and empowerment continues to this day, and its history speaks volumes about the power of a single beauty product.

Red lipstick has been a symbol of resistance and empowerment throughout history, and its use continues to unite people in the fight for equality.

Ada Hsieh (pronounced Aye-duh Shay) is the CEO and Founder of Fluency Beauty - a plant-based makeup brand colored from...well plants. Fluency Beauty offers multipurpose beauty sticks colored from vegetables like beets and potatoes for eyes, lips, and face providing buildable color for seamless blends of ease and efficiency.

www.fluencybeauty.com
ada@adalipbeauty.com

DIGITAL MEDIA MARKETING SERVICES PACKAGES

SOCIAL MEDIA MANAGEMENT

STANDARD

$700 USD/Mo

- Social Media (15 Social Posts per month) for 2 networks
- 8 custom Images per month
- M, W, F post comment monitoring
- Monthly Analytics Reports

PREMIUM

- Social Media (30 Social Posts per month) for 3 networks
- 10 custom Images per month
- Daily comment monitoring
- Monthly Analytics Reports

$999 USD/Mo

GOLD

$1500 USD/Mo

- Social Media (45 Social Posts per month) for 4 networks.
- 15 custom Images per month
- Daily comment monitoring
- Monthly Analytics Reports

JDCONSULTINGSOLUTIONS.COM

FASHION VISIONARIES
Shaping Style and Sustainability

by Belinda Jane

In the annals of fashion history, there are luminaries whose names are etched in the fabric of time. These women, visionaries ahead of their time, not only shaped the course of fashion but also paved the way for future generations of designers and entrepreneurs.

THOSE WHO PAVED THE WAY

Gabrielle "Coco" Chanel, often hailed as one of the most influential figures in 20th-century fashion, revolutionized women's clothing with her timeless designs. Rejecting the restrictive corsets and embellished gowns of her era, Chanel championed simplicity, elegance, and functionality. Her iconic little black dress, quilted handbags, and tweed suits became synonymous with modernity and sophistication, forever changing the landscape of fashion.

Elsa Schiaparelli, the irreverent Italian designer known for her bold and surreal creations, challenged conventions with her avant-garde aesthetic. From her iconic lobster dress to her collaboration with Salvador Dalí on whimsical designs, Schiaparelli pushed the boundaries of fashion, blurring the lines between art and couture. Her fearless approach to design continues to inspire creatives to this day.

By Elsa Schiaparelli - Original publication: Worn by Wallis Simpson in February 1937Immediate source: https://www.philamuseum.org/collections/permanent/65327.html, Fair use, https://en.wikipedia.org/w/index.php?curid=66752744

MADELEINE VIONNET

By Berko gallery - Own work, CC BY-SA 4.0, https://commons.wikimedia.org/w/index.php?curid=94077642

Madeleine Vionnet, often referred to as the "architect of fashion," pioneered revolutionary techniques in draping and bias-cutting that transformed the way garments fit and flowed on the body. With her masterful craftsmanship and attention to detail, Vionnet created garments that celebrated the natural curves of women, rejecting the rigid structures of traditional tailoring. Her innovative approach to design earned her a place among the pantheon of fashion greats.

By Jeanne Lanvin - Own work Photo taken at Catwalk exhibition at Rijksmuseum, March 2016, Public Domain, https://commons.wikimedia.org/w/index.php?curid=54657219

Jeanne Lanvin, the visionary French designer who founded one of the oldest surviving fashion houses, left an indelible mark on the world of fashion with her romantic and feminine creations. Lanvin's intricate embroideries, delicate fabrics, and meticulous attention to detail captured the hearts of women around the world, solidifying her legacy as a pioneer of modern luxury fashion.

These women, and many others like them, were trailblazers in an industry dominated by men. Through their creativity, resilience, and determination, they shattered glass ceilings and paved the way for future generations of female designers and entrepreneurs. Their legacies serve as a reminder of the power of fashion to empower, inspire, and uplift women from all walks of life.

Before the era of fast fashion, craftsmanship and quality reigned supreme. Garments were meticulously crafted by skilled artisans, often using natural fibers such as cotton, wool, and silk. Each piece was a labor of love, designed to withstand the test of time both in terms of durability and style. Women were discerning consumers, investing in pieces that would serve them for years to come rather than fleeting trends that would fade with the seasons.

The shift towards mass-produced, fast fashion marked a seismic change in the industry. Overseas manufacturing hubs churned out clothing at breakneck speed, flooding the market with cheap, disposable garments. While this offered affordability and accessibility to consumers, it came at a steep cost to both people and planet.

The fast fashion revolution brought with it a host of environmental and ethical issues. Pollution from manufacturing processes poisoned waterways and polluted the air, while the overuse of water and reliance on synthetic fibers exacerbated the strain on our planet's resources. The rise of fast fashion also saw an alarming increase in the exploitation of garment workers, with many subjected to unsafe working conditions and unfair wages.

As awareness of these issues grows, so too does the call for change. Now, more than ever, there is a need to return to the 'old ways' of prioritizing quality over quantity in fashion. Investing in well-made garments crafted from natural fibers not only ensures longevity and versatility but also benefits both our health and the health of the planet.

Natural fibers such as organic cotton, linen, and wool offer numerous advantages over their synthetic counterparts. Not only are they biodegradable, reducing the burden on landfills, but they also require less energy and water to produce. Additionally, natural fibers are breathable and hypoallergenic, making them gentle on the skin and reducing the risk of allergic reactions.

By prioritizing quality over quantity, we can reduce our environmental footprint and support ethical practices within the fashion industry. Choosing garments that are built to last not only reduces the need for constant consumption but also allows us to reconnect with the stories woven into each piece. Fashion becomes more than just a fleeting trend – it becomes a statement of values and a commitment to a more sustainable future.

As we navigate the complexities of an ever-changing world, let us remember the lessons of the past and strive for a future where fashion is both beautiful and ethical. By embracing quality over quantity, we can weave a more sustainable and equitable world for generations to come.

Get your new

Use promo code
SHETALKS30 for 30% OFF

A JOURNEY OF
Faith & Endurance

The Remarkable Saga of Alice Walsh Strong

By Andrea Bell

Growing up in Utah, the tales of pioneers were woven into the fabric of my childhood. Little did I realize that the gripping narratives of these pioneers were not just stories but the lived experiences of my own family. Moved by the heartbreaking story of the woman who buried her son and husband in shallow graves along the frozen trail, later revealed to be my great-grandmother. Who once lived in the home where I spent my childhood, the home that my parents now own. This is the incredible story of Alice Walsh Strong, a woman I am proud and blessed to call my own, whose resilience, positivity, and unwavering faith defy the odds.

Photo Credits By Lewis Hine - U.S. National Archives and Records Administration, Public Domain, https://commons.wikimedia.org/w/index.php?curid=16896786

Photo Source: Wikimedia Commons

In the heart of England's Industrial Revolution, a young mill girl named Alice toiled in the cotton mills of Lancashire. Her life took a profound turn when she heard the teachings of missionaries from America, sparking a newfound hope and faith in her heart. Against all odds, she embraced this new religion, The Church of Jesus Christ of Latter Day Saints, ultimately leading her on a remarkable journey of faith, sacrifice, and endurance.

As Alice married William Walsh and started a family, the call to gather to Zion resonated within her. Together with their three young children, they embarked on a perilous journey with the Martin Handcart Company of 1856, crossing the stormy Atlantic to fulfill their divine calling. Little did they know that this journey would test their faith and resilience to the limits.

Embarking on the westward journey with a handcart was a test of endurance and fortitude for pioneers. Opting for a more economical yet arduous route, they navigated the unforgiving terrain with two-wheeled carts laden with their possessions. The rhythmic trundle of wheels and determined footsteps

Photo Credits Glen Hawkins, Courtesy of Museum of Utah Art History

Photo Source: Wikimedia Commons

echoed the challenges faced by those pulling the carts themselves. The physical toll was palpable as they persevered through harsh conditions. In the vein of the Walsh family's resilience, these handcart pioneers etched a poignant chapter in the larger narrative of westward expansion, leaving an enduring legacy of courage and determination on the untamed canvas of the American frontier. Alice Walsh Strong's story stands as a testament to the indomitable spirit of those who braved the unknown, exemplifying that faith and endurance can triumph over even the harshest of trials.

In the unforgiving embrace of a Wyoming winter, Alice Walsh Strong found herself huddled with her two children under a snow-covered handcart at Devil's Gate. With her husband, William, standing guard against the perils of the night, and the biting cold intensifying, Alice reflected on the hardships that led her to this dire moment. The trek from Liverpool to Winter Quarters was arduous, plagued by storms and a measles outbreak. Tragedy struck when all three children succumbed to illness during the Atlantic crossing, the oldest Robert being stricken most severely.

Arriving in the Winter Quarters, they faced a scarcity of materials and no means to sustain themselves over the winter, forcing them to join a handcart company led by Captain Edward Martin. Unprepared, Alice and William faced the harsh reality of prairie life as they pulled and pushed their handcart through the rugged terrain, enduring bitter cold and rationed supplies. Alice spoke of grown men driven to tears from the lack of nourishment. She reflects on the passing of her oldest son recalling being so stricken with grief was unable to recall where he was buried.

"My husband died at Devil's Gate. The ground was frozen so hard the morning he died that they could not dig a grave. I think they must have put him under the snow. Nine others died the same night. This left me alone to care for my two children. The boy [John, age 3] became so weak that he could not stand alone. I had to sit and hold both children nearly all the time. When we came to a place where we could go no further and I had no exercise, my shoes froze to my feet. Later when I was able to remove them, the skin and flesh came off too, leaving only the bones. My hands were severely frozen."

In the heart of Wyoming, where the Sweetwater River carved through mountains, Alice's plight reached its height. Snowed in at Devil's Gate, she faced the stark reality of being a widow. Now left to care for her children in brutal conditions.

By Unknown author - Utah State Historical Society Classified Photo Collection Title: Joseph A. Young Identifier: 39222001410682Photo Number: 14279, Public Domain, https://commons.wikimedia.org/w/index.php?curid=11842078

Help finally arrived in the form of Joseph A. Young from the Salt Lake Valley, marking a turning point for Alice and her children. Their arrival in Salt Lake City on November 30, 1856, marked the end of a treacherous journey. Doctors did their best with her badly frozen feet so that she may still be able to walk, marking the beginning of a new life.

Life in the Salt Lake Valley presented fresh challenges, but Alice found solace living among the Saints, guided by Prophet Brigham Young. Despite the sacrifices and hardships, Alice's resilience shone through. Her family, taken in by the Strong family, became an example of the strength and unity fostered within the community.

As Alice's life in Utah unfolds, so does the state's transformation—witnessing the joining of the Transcontinental Railroad, the struggle for statehood, and the changing landscape of a burgeoning community. Weathering the storms of life, including the grasshopper plague and the great famine, later forced from their homes and possessions to move south due to threats from the army. Alice related "times were hard there, and it was very difficult to find enough to eat."

Most of the time, life was just working hard to have enough for her family to eat and keep them clothed. All her children learned at an early age how to help with the cooking, in the garden, gathering wild fruits and berries, and to find odd jobs to bring in a little money for the family. Alice was industrious and creative in providing for her family and contributing to the Relief Society organization-serving.

Alice, amidst all the hardship lived a full and enjoyable life and married and had three more children. She enjoyed life and motherhood. In her later years, Alice, known as Grandma Strong, became a revered figure in North Ogden. Her life was marked by enduring friendships, celebrations, and the passing of an era as statehood dawned. The story culminates with Alice's passing at the age of 96, leaving behind a legacy of faith, sacrifice, and an unshakable belief in the gospel.

Alice's testimony echoes through the generations, urging her descendants to recognize her sacrifices, hold strong to their faith, and work for the sake of the gospel. Her life, intertwined with the history of Utah, serves as an inspiration—a testament to the indomitable spirit that guided her through the Refiner's fire.

Yes, tragedy struck on the frozen plains of Wyoming, where Alice lost her husband and eldest son. Yet, instead of succumbing to despair, her story became a testament to faith, obedience, and unwavering determination.

Alice's journey is encapsulated in her own words: "I am thankful that the Lord preserved my life and made it possible for me to gather to Zion. Jesus said, 'Unless we forsake father and mother, houses and lands, for His sake, we are not worthy of Him.' This I have done for Him... I left my loved ones and all those dear to me in England. I have passed through many trials but have never regretted coming to Zion." Her testimony reflects the sacrifices made and the profound faith that sustained her through adversity.

Alice's remarkable story encapsulates the unwavering spirit of a pioneer—navigating the Industrial Revolution's challenges, embracing a newfound faith, enduring the hardships of the handcart journey, and finding strength in the Salt Lake Valley. "A Journey of Faith…" stands as a testament to Alice Walsh Strong's indomitable spirit and the resilience of those who embarked on the arduous journey to build a new life in the American West.

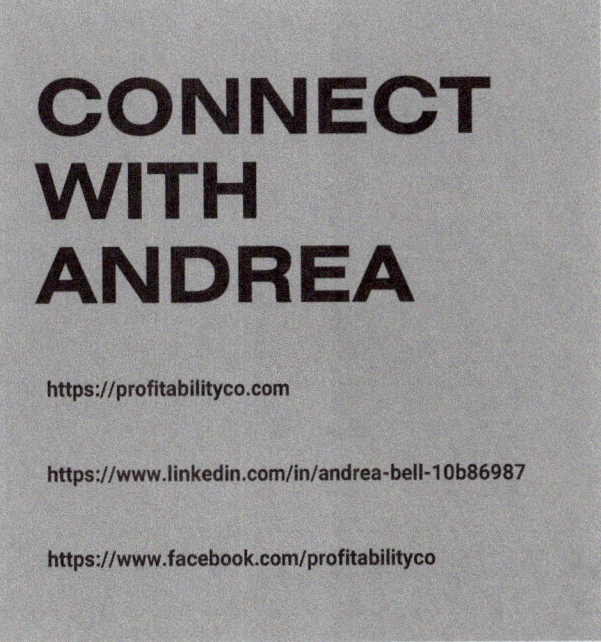

CONNECT WITH ANDREA

https://profitabilityco.com

https://www.linkedin.com/in/andrea-bell-10b86987

https://www.facebook.com/profitabilityco

FEATURED ARTICLE

RUSHIA BROWN
Growing Up WNBA

By Tia Cristy

G rowing up in South Carolina, she didn't touch a basketball until her sophomore year of high school. That might not sound like such a big deal for some young girls out there, but it is impressive as can be when you learn that we are talking about retired WNBA star, Rushia Brown.

I had the great pleasure to sit and talk with this 6'2" beauty and learn all about her family and career, from her basketball glory days to currently making a global impact with helping young women on and off the court and supporting the wellbeing of sports retirees.

In the spring of 1972, Rushia was born in the Bronx, New York, but three years later, her parents decided to move to an area where riding bikes wouldn't be so dangerous, contending with busy streets. Rushia grew up in Summerville, SC, where she started from humble beginnings, surrounded by her very tight-knit family.

"Family is everything," she says. "I'm the oldest of three siblings. I have a kick-ass sister who just retired as one of the top-ranking officers in the Navy. I have a brother who's an artist with his own art gallery. We are three very, very, ...very different people, but there's that core: the hard work, the belief in family, and the love we all have for what we do. It's that core that we have consistent."

FAMILY VALUES

The family unit was strong since conception and wonderfully remains that way still today. However, Rushia's world crumbled around her when she was in the midst of her freshman year of high school when her beloved father, who had been ill for some time, tragically passed away.

"I was a 'daddy's girl'... He was a huge sports fan," she says with admiration. "I wasn't into it then," she admits. "He actually wanted me to be a singer," she says with disbelief, "I don't know why. I couldn't sing."

Of course, she had childhood ideas and aspirations, but when Rushia's father became ill, any potential dreams understandably fell by the wayside. She found herself automatically in the role of primary 'caregiver' since her mother had to work to keep the family fed and dressed. She remembers clearly, as a young girl, pushing her father's pain medication as she sat in front of me on our video chat, drawing imaginary lines in the air as she explained to me how she had to inject him to ease his agony.

Everything Changes

Rushia explains that she was always a good girl up until then. Neighbors and teachers alike witnessed the change and watched the light grow dim on this ray of sunshine. Fortunately, they did their best to protect and help a broken-hearted girl during her grief.

Then and there, Summerville's girls' basketball coach asked Rushia to play for the school's Junior varsity. Rushia's mom agreed it was a great idea, and Rushia knew it was time to make a conscious change in a positive direction.

"Basketball was how my family brought me back. My dad loved basketball," she remembers. "After I tried it, I loved it, too!"

And, yes, Rushia may have fallen in love with basketball, but the bonus is that she was also extraordinary at it. By the time she reached her senior year at Summerville High School, Rushia was one of the top prospects for colleges nationwide. She was recruited by Harvard, Chapel Hill, and Duke, but when it came time to decide, Rushia chose Furman University because she wanted to remain close to her mother.

"My mom and I have always had an amazing relationship. She lives with me now in my home in Atlanta," she says.

The love and passion that flows from Rushia as she speaks about her mother and how this 78-year-old go-getter, who is still moving and shaking after all these glorious years, still inspires her.
"She showed me what work was," Rushia says. "She didn't stop until the job was done, which has affected my life tremendously. Still, to this day, I know how to work. If I have stuff to do, I'll get up at three o'clock in the morning to do it. I might have only gone to bed at midnight (because I'm in bed by midnight. I'd rather get up early.), but I'll be up at three or four to make sure I'm getting this work done."

So, it's no surprise that Rushia's journey in basketball was marked by a relentless pursuit of excellence both on and off the court. After making her mark in high school basketball, she was off to achieve greatness at the collegiate level, and there's no doubt she left an indelible mark on the sport.

College Accolades

During her time at Furman, Rushia distinguished herself as one of the most dominant players in the nation. Her exceptional talent and work ethic propelled her to the top of the college basketball world, earning her numerous accolades and honors along the way. Rushia's collegiate career was nothing short of remarkable, from being named Southern Conference Freshman of the Year to earning multiple MVP awards and Southern Conference Player of the Year honors.

Perhaps the crowning achievement of her college career came when her jersey, emblazoned with the number 34, was retired. This honor served as a testament to her unparalleled contributions to the program and solidified her legacy as one of the all-time greats in University history.

Leaving on a Jet Plane

Following her illustrious collegiate career, Rushia set her sights on the professional ranks, where she would continue to make waves on the international stage. Over the course of a decade, Rushia's professional career took her to five different countries, including Spain, France, Italy, Greece, and Korea. Her tenure overseas showcased her versatility and adaptability as a player, as she thrived in various basketball cultures and leagues. Not to mention, this extraordinary woman learned the languages of the countries that she lived in.

"I love learning about people," she says, "And you can do that when you know the language."

She Hits the Big Time

In addition to her success overseas, Rushia also made her mark in the Women's National Basketball Association (WNBA), where she spent seven memorable seasons. She became one of the first players to sign with the newly formed organization. During her remarkable time in the WNBA, she wore the jerseys of two franchises, the Cleveland Rockers and the Charlotte Sting. Throughout her seven-year tenure in the league, she continued to showcase her scoring prowess, rebounding ability, and shot-blocking abilities, earning the respect of teammates, opponents, and fans alike. But above all else,

"BASKETBALL MADE ME FEEL A CLOSER BOND TO MY DAD"

OFF
the
Court

Beyond her on-court exploits, Rushia's impact extended far beyond basketball arenas. She served as a role model and mentor to countless aspiring athletes, using her platform to inspire and empower others to pursue their dreams, which she still does to this day. Whether she was hosting basketball clinics, participating in community outreach programs, or advocating for social causes, Brown remained committed to making a positive difference in the lives of those around her.

"Community is so important," she tells me. "I love getting out there in the community and making a positive impact."

Today, in the world of basketball, it's safe to say that Rushia Brown's legacy continues to inspire a new generation of athletes to reach for the stars and chase their dreams. Her unwavering dedication to excellence, both on and off the court, serves as a shining example of what can be achieved through hard work, determination, and a passion for the game. As basketball continues to evolve and grow, Rushia's impact is an enduring legacy that transcends the sport.

After her retirement, Rushia decided to continue to invest in people. She transitioned from being a professional player to pursuing her passions to continue on a stream of positive impact.

Back to the Books

Her journey (so far) has been one of ambition, leadership, and empowerment. Armed with a thirst for knowledge, she pursued her Executive MBA from George Washington University to fortify her capabilities for her entrepreneurial and future endeavors. And driven by that entrepreneurial spirit and desire to make a positive impact, she embarked on passionate missions across various domains.

New Transitions

One of her most notable contributions is the establishment of the Women's Professional Basketball Alumnae, a pioneering organization dedicated to supporting female athletes transitioning from the realm of professional basketball into mainstream society.

"I'm an empath, and I've also been able to learn from my experiences," she says.
With first-hand recognition of the challenges these athletes face, Rushia sought to provide a support network and resources to facilitate a smooth transition into post-athletic life.

In addition to her work with the Alumnae, she co-founded ServCom, a nonprofit organization committed to enhancing communities through educational and enrichment programs. Through ServCom, she aimed to address societal needs and foster positive change by empowering individuals with knowledge and skills to thrive in their communities. Another program she created is BAWSE GIRLS. It is a groundbreaking initiative designed to empower young women by equipping them with the necessary tools to cultivate self-esteem, self-respect, and self-worth. Through this program, participants are encouraged to develop positive attitudes toward goal setting and achievement.

She tells me a heart-wrenching story of one young girl caught in a dangerous web of generational curses.

"I made her my project. She was great," she says with passion pouring out of her soul. But as she dives into the deep details of this young girl's generational challenge, I see the look change on Rushia's face. "She stopped showing up."

It turns out not everyone is ready to embrace the love, support, and guidance of these community programs, but for every one person who's not ready, there are a dozen who are, and Rushia is prepared to take them in. I asked her if it stemmed from the love and support she got from her community when she was going through her rough time as a young girl.

"Absolutely!" she says. "Absolutely, it was pinnacle. And I want to be there for these girls."

Momma Ru

Rushia has a beautiful maternal instinct, which she showcases not only with youths in the community but with her lovely daughter, Morgan. When I mention Morgan, Rushia gushes.

"My daughter is my everything. She changed me for the better," she smiles.

Besides caring for the kids, Rushia also continues to care for other members of the community while applying her entrepreneurial skills and combining her hobby-passion of cooking. Her ventures now extend into the culinary realm by establishing Hearts & Hands Catering. Together with her family, she created a yummy business that provides nutritious alternatives to the community and promotes healthy living and holistic wellness.

"YOU MAY FIND THAT MAKING A DIFFERENCE FOR OTHERS MAKES THE BIGGEST DIFFERENCE IN YOU."
— BRIAN WILLIAMS

MAKING BLACK HISTORY

Another family business emerged when her brother and she spearheaded the creation of Young Black Entrepreneur Magazine, a quarterly publication designed to inspire and educate minorities on entrepreneurship. The magazine catalyzes aspiring business owners to embark on their entrepreneurial journey with confidence by sharing stories of successful entrepreneurs and providing valuable insights and resources.

Rushia sounded emotional as she told me a story about her mother giving a keynote speech over Zoom for Black History Month. Her mother spoke in a packed Zoom room on her history of growing up on a plantation. Rushia's grandparents were sharecroppers, and as her mother shared her childhood with the room, her mother spoke of how their family was one step away from slavery because they didn't receive close to what they deserved. There wasn't a dry eye in the chat room as she shared stories of what she had experienced and seen all those years ago.
"It told me so much about why she is the way she is," she says admiringly. "I knew some things, but now it makes sense."

As children, we tend to know a one-dimensional version of our parents, but it's impressive when we discover they are multifaceted.
"I can understand what my daughter must think about me because I am a product of my mother. It just makes sense," she explains.

FEATURING
RUSHIA BROWN

A New Mission Formed

The whole experience and enlightenment that came from Rushia watching her mother inspired another project called Mommy and Me, which will focus on the relationships between mothers and daughters.

"I've played basketball professionally for 17 years. I'll give my daughter advice, and she'll be like, 'Oh, mom!' But we go into the local gym, and she's listening to some guy who's shooting airballs," she scoffs. "But I get it, I'm her mother! So, the program will teach these relationships to look at one another and help build them," she explains.

Rushia is still building relationships within the WNBA as well. During her tenure in the WNBA, spanning over five years, she assumed roles in executive management that showcased her leadership acumen and passion for positive change. Beginning with her tenure at the NBA/WNBA headquarters in New York through the Crossover Program, Brown gained invaluable experience and insights into the inner workings of professional sports organizations.

Changing History

In 2010, after a celebrity game, Rushia became aware that one of her WNBA 'sisters' was, in fact, homeless. Rushia was shocked and devastated by this news. On a mission, she had contacted the organization and found there was no help for retired women players. She then moved on to reaching out to NBRPA, which is the association for retired athletes. At that time, they only helped male athletes. But once Rushia and her fellow 'sisters' were done, women were added into the retiree association.

And I'm beyond happy to announce that just days before this interview, Rushia Brown was brought on as the association's newest member of the Board of Directors.

Can't Stop Won't Stop

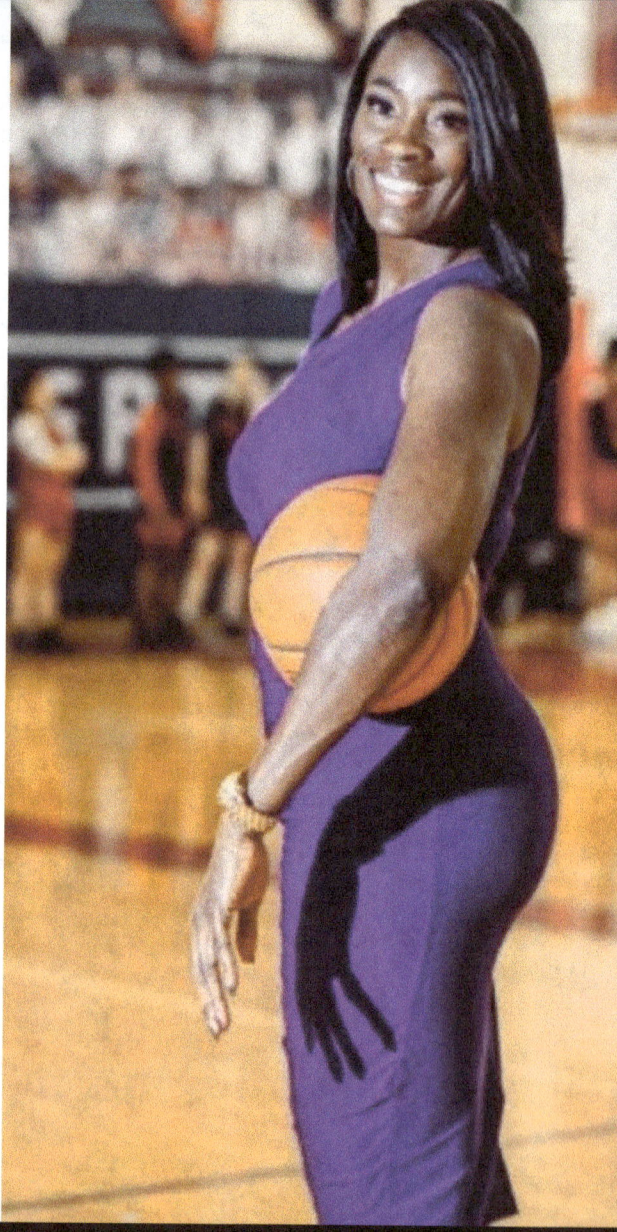

On that note, Rushia is an impossible force to ignore, and you wouldn't want to, either. Her beautiful soul and generous heart radiate light from this superstar, and you just can't help but want to be part of her world. The magic she had brought to the court is the same that she brings to the rest of the world. She keeps a hold on the athletics realm as well as being a mentor throughout communities.

In 2018, Rushia played a pivotal role in the relocation of the San Antonio Silver Stars to Las Vegas, where she served as the Player Programs & Franchise Development Manager for two years with the Las Vegas Aces. Her strategic vision and dedication contributed to the team's success and growth within the Las Vegas community. Subsequently, she transitioned to the role of Director of Community Relations and Youth Sports for the Los Angeles Sparks, where she continued to champion positive change and community engagement. Through her initiatives, she inspired individuals to pursue their passions and strive for excellence, both on and off the court.

In every endeavor, Rushia Brown exemplifies resilience, vision, and a commitment to uplifting others. Her multifaceted career serves as a testament to the power of determination and leadership in effecting positive change in communities and industries alike. And the love for her family and the efforts she puts forth in her own community should be an inspiration to us all.

About Author Tia Cristy

The most important thing about Tia is her way of cutting through the white noise and oversaturation of data to provide the most efficient and trusted information to others. Tia has been a radio personality for over 20 years. She's the founder of Tips from Tia and CEO of Ready Speaker One, as well as an International Best-selling author, national speaker, and TedX alumni. She has humbly earned the title of Personality and Tips Expert in Health, Family, Lifestyle, Home, and Beauty through radio, television, and print.

A LEAGUE OF THEIR OWN

By Dr. Julie Ducharme

Hopefully, you have seen and remember the iconic movie A League of Their Own, starring Geena Davis and Tom Hanks, with the memorable line, "There is no crying in baseball." This movie, based on a true story, depicts how the women's baseball league came about during wartime. I was fortunate enough to meet one of these women from the iconic league. It's not often that one gets to meet someone who played such an important role in history. I had the privilege of meeting and talking with Lil Faralla, a pioneer in women's sports and an integral part of US history. As someone who played sports in college and at the higher level, I never truly considered the women who paved the way for athletes like myself. Lil Faralla is part of an iconic group of women who played in the first-ever women's professional baseball league, the All-American Girls Professional Baseball League. I was privileged that Lil gave me some time to talk with her about her experiences in sports and more. Lil, at 92 years young when I interviewed her, is one of the last 3 surviving women who played in this league.

An interview with *"the"* Lil Faralla

Getting Into Sports

I grew up playing baseball with the boys and loved sports. This opened the door for me to play professionally. I was paid a dollar a week to drive to LA and play with professional teams.

Recruited for the Professional League

A scout came to watch me, and I was sent a telegram to come and try out for the team. So I went and tried out. I figured, why not?

Memorable Moments

My most memorable moments are when I pitched 2 no-hitters and when I was inducted into the Hall of Fame.

Accuracy of "A League of Their Own"

"There's no crying in baseball!" That was what we said, and the movie was pretty accurate. I was a consultant on the movie and worked with the actors to ensure its accuracy.

Life Beyond Baseball

After baseball, I worked with the Los Angeles Police Department as a Sheriff for 20 years. I saw many things and even worked on the Manson case.

Little-Known Fact

I joined the Coast Guard before age 17, and my mother had to sign off on my paperwork because I was not old enough.

REFLECTIONS

While America was in the middle of World War II, baseball was at risk. It was during this time that women, who were frowned upon for even wearing pants, let alone playing baseball, stepped up to help keep America's spirits up. Becoming a beacon of hope, these women provided an escape from war worries and concerns, paving the way for women like myself to have opportunities to play sports.

Lil said,

"You know, I never looked at myself as being any different from men playing the sport. I was a woman, yes, but I just loved to play ball, and that was all I needed to be successful, is a love for the game and love for what I do. If you love what you do, you will be successful."

Since this article, Lil has passed on, but if I could give any advice, it would be to meet with women like Lil who were out paving the way. Her insight was phenomenal, and her outlook on life was tremendous. She had no regrets. She loved that she played baseball, joined the Coast Guard, and was a sheriff. She lived life to the fullest in some of the most male-dominated worlds.

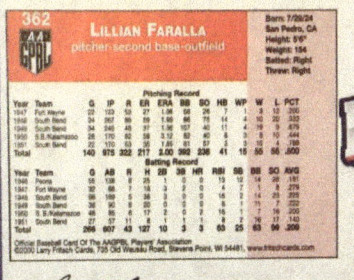

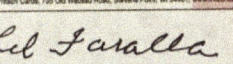

Navigating Empowerment

*E*mbark on a captivating journey through the life of Carolyn Leighton, the brilliant mind behind WITI (Women in Technology International)*. Growing up amid the cultural tapestry of Providence, Rhode Island, Carolyn found herself in a landscape of opinions and judgments – what she lovingly refers to as the land of critics and judges. In this series of conversations, I, Luba Sakharuk, delve into Carolyn's experiences, reflecting on shared Jewish heritage, cultural influences, and the evolution of WITI.

*Although WITI underwent a rebranding from Women in Technology International to Workforce, Innovation, Trust, and Influence in 2023, it became evident during the interview that the commitment to diversity had been included Carolyn's vision from day one.

WRITTEN BY
LUBA SAKHARUK

Part 1:

EMBRACING CHALLENGES AND BUILDING NETWORKS

Join me, as I share a snippet of my personal journey while chatting with the inspiring Carolyn Leighton, Founder of WITI Organization.

My journey began as a wide-eyed 14-year-old from Lithuania, setting foot in the United States. College posed unexpected challenges, especially since English wasn't my forte at the time. Fast forward to a pivotal moment – I met my husband at 18, who subtly planted the idea that computer science could be my calling. Intrigued by my love for math and with a heart full of love, I switched to a computer science degree, taking a leap of faith with zero confidence.

In a heartwarming conversation, Carolyn Leighton expressed admiration for the positive influence my husband had on my life choices. We delved into the hurdles faced in computer science classes and explored the nuanced perception of intelligence. Carolyn shared insights from a twin study, shedding light on the significant genetic influence on behavior and intelligence.

Our discussion extended to overcoming fears and the transformative power of mentorship programs. Inspired by my own journey, I initiated a mentorship program to support those grappling with doubts about their capabilities. Carolyn, drawing from her experiences, highlighted the game-changing impact of networks in her own career.

In this tech-driven world, we're all navigating our unique paths, and it's essential to recognize that challenges don't define our intelligence. As I reflect on my journey, I encourage you to embrace the difficulties, cultivate mentorship connections, and leverage the strength found in supportive networks.

Tech journeys are as diverse as the individuals embarking on them, and by sharing our stories, we empower others to overcome obstacles and reach for the stars. Here's to embracing challenges, fostering mentorship, and building a network that propels us to new heights in the world of technology!

Part 2:

UNVEILING THE POWER OF NETWORKS AND DIVERSE PERSPECTIVES IN TECH

Carolyn Leighton, Founder of WITI Organization, eloquently pointed out that beyond our psychological insecurities, we all possess a unique genetic list dictating what we know, what we can do, and even what we think we can't do. It's a reminder that our differences don't define our intelligence; instead, they contribute to the richness of our perspectives.

Our discussion took a fascinating turn as Carolyn shared her journey with WITI and the realization that collaboration and networks are paramount. Her revelation resonated deeply with me, echoing my own experiences that inspired me to initiate a mentorship program.

In my pursuit to contribute to the tech community, I embarked on a six-month experiment, bringing together a diverse group of about 10 women every Tuesday through Zoom. What began as a tech-centric idea evolved into a melting pot of professionals from various fields – lawyers, artists, accountants – united by a common goal of supporting and learning from each other.

Carolyn mirrored my sentiments about the power of networks, recounting her journey with WITI. It struck a chord as she emphasized the mistake she made early in her career, assuming she had to do everything alone. Her revelation about the strength found in a network of like-minded women resonated with me on a profound level.

As I continued the mentorship program, a beautiful realization unfolded. The diversity within our group became a wellspring of innovative solutions. A lawyer's perspective complemented a scientist's, an artist's creativity inspired an accountant, and we found that shared challenges transcended industries.

Our conversation delved into the early days of WITI, with Carolyn sharing a brilliant model inspired by diverse groups at Hewlett Packard. The idea of bringing together individuals from different backgrounds, each contributing a unique perspective, became the essence of WITI's vision.

Carolyn's journey, peppered with experiences from the late '80s, resonated with the evolution I witnessed in the tech world. Our paths may differ, but the essence of our stories remains the same – embracing challenges, fostering mentorship, and building networks are catalysts for personal and professional growth.

As Carolyn and I exchanged insights, it became clear that the magic lies in embracing our differences, learning from one another, and collectively propelling the tech industry forward. Stay tuned for more conversations, insights, and tech tales as we navigate the ever-evolving landscape of technology together.

Cheers to collaboration, mentorship, and the incredible power of diverse networks!

> "I get the wonderful pleasure of hearing from many women about how WITI has hade a difference for them. That, for me, is greater than any award I could receive."

Part 3:

EMBRACING UNIQUENESS: A JOURNEY OF EMPOWERMENT IN THE TECH WORLD

Let us continue in our exploration of the power of networks and diverse perspectives in the tech industry, alongside the remarkable Carolyn Leighton, Founder of WITI (as of 2023, rebranded to Workforce, Innovation, Trust and Influence) Organization.

Our conversation took an insightful turn as Carolyn touched upon something that resonated deeply with both of us – the tendency to feel that something is wrong with us when we're not aware of certain aspects of ourselves. This shared experience echoed through our lives, highlighting the universal nature of this perception.

Carolyn emphasized that this feeling isn't limited to moments of unawareness; it extends to how children, especially those who are different or unique, perceive themselves based on how others experience them. It struck a chord with me, as I reflected on the countless individuals, I've encountered in the tech world who, much like Carolyn and me, felt like the odd ones out.

As Carolyn embarked on the journey of creating WITI, she discovered a community of men and women who shared similar sentiments growing up – feeling odd, different, and reluctant to join groups or sororities. The realization was both heartening and eye-opening. Many, like us, assumed they couldn't fit into any group due to their perceived uniqueness.

While the sentiment may carry a tinge of sadness, Carolyn and I see it as an intriguing aspect of the human experience. Life deals us a hand, and it's our choice how we play it. The realization that it's our choice to embrace our uniqueness and take control of our narrative is both empowering and liberating.

Yet, Carolyn shared a valuable insight – with this empowerment comes the responsibility to remind ourselves and each other not to succumb to the victim mentality. Society, often unconsciously, perpetuates stereotypes and challenges women, making it crucial for us to support and uplift one another.

Our conversation delved into the complex nature of societal perceptions, touching upon the delicate balance between challenging the status quo and inadvertently reinforcing stereotypes. Carolyn's reflections on the feminist movements of the past added depth to our discussion, highlighting the dual nature of societal change – sometimes a good shakeup is necessary, but it comes with its challenges.

As we navigate the intricate landscape of the tech world, Carolyn and I invite you to join us on this journey of empowerment and self-discovery. It's time to celebrate our uniqueness, embrace the responsibility of choice, and build a supportive community that thrives on diversity.

Stay tuned for more insights, shared experiences, and empowering tales from the tech trenches. Let's continue to champion each other and shape a future where our differences are not perceived as limitations but as strengths.

Cheers to embracing our uniqueness and creating a tech world where everyone has a seat at the table!

Part 4:

NAVIGATING CHALLENGES, EMBRACING HERITAGE: A TALE OF RESILIENCE IN TECH

Our dialogue took an unexpected yet poignant turn as Carolyn inquired about my family's journey to America. The question unraveled a chapter of my life filled with challenges, resilience, and a deep connection to my roots.

In response to Carolyn's question about my family joining me in America, I shared a bittersweet tale. Unfortunately, my father and grandmother chose to stay behind, making the separation endure for 28 long years. Each vacation became an opportunity to bridge the distance, with heartfelt visits to my homeland. Though my dad and grandmother are no longer with us, the memories of those visits and the enduring connection remain etched in my heart.

Carolyn expressed genuine interest in my memoir, a testament to the power of storytelling. My memoir, a labor of love, delves into the complexities of my family's journey, the challenges faced, and the enduring spirit that shaped me into the person I am today.

Our shared experiences of feeling different and questioning ourselves struck a chord. Carolyn beautifully articulated how societal perceptions, especially in childhood, can lead us to believe that something is wrong with us. We explored the transformative nature of challenges, with Carolyn emphasizing that the most profound lessons often emerge from the difficult ones.

The conversation seamlessly transitioned into Carolyn sharing her family's history – her parents escaping antisemitism, meeting at the University of Michigan, and the amalgamation of diverse backgrounds. It resonated deeply with me, connecting me to the vast tapestry of immigrant experiences.

As Carolyn reflected on appreciating her family's business acumen, it prompted a discussion on the importance of understanding our roots and sharing those stories. My memoir, crafted for my children, serves as a legacy of my grandparents' struggles and triumphs. We agreed that stories carry not just personal history but also lessons for future generations.

The topic of entitlement arose, prompting a thoughtful discussion on instilling appreciation and a strong work ethic in our children. Carolyn emphasized the value of encouraging service and volunteering, instilling a sense of compassion and humility.

Our conversation wrapped up on a profound note – life is a journey, and every twist and turn shapes us into who we are meant to be. As we navigate the tech landscape, let's celebrate our unique journeys, cherish our heritage, and foster compassion in the ever-evolving world of technology.

Part 5:

EMPOWERING WOMEN, CULTIVATING CONNECTIONS: UNVEILING THE MAGIC OF WITI

In our ongoing conversation, I had the pleasure of engaging with Carolyn Leighton, the visionary founder of WITI (Workforce, Innovation, Trust and Influence) originally known as (Women in Technology International) Organization in an insightful dialogue on networking, knowledge-sharing, and the transformative connections fostered by WITI.

Our discussion took an exciting turn as I shared my involvement with "SheTalks," a magazine dedicated to supporting women veterans, led by a remarkable woman committed to making a difference. Intrigued by her selfless endeavors, I eagerly accepted the opportunity to lead the Women in Technology section of the magazine. This initiative seamlessly aligns with WITI's mission of spotlighting the incredible achievements of women in the tech industry.

As we explored the significance of Women's History Month, my thoughts turned to Carolyn's inspiring journey and the profound impact WITI has had on countless lives. I couldn't help but express my excitement about the potential of WITI and Carolyn's insights. Feeling a deep connection, I mentioned my anticipation of continuing our engaging discussions over dinner during my next visit to the West Coast, as I believed Carolyn and I could talk for hours.

Carolyn, appreciative and flattered, echoed the sentiment and expressed gratitude for the recognition. We discussed the transformative nature of WITI, not just in terms of professional growth but also in broadening perspectives and fostering a sense of community.

The conversation seamlessly transitioned into the strategic importance of diversity in thought and experiences. Carolyn, in a heartfelt request, suggested writing an article on the magical process of WITI, emphasizing the psychological development it brings by looking beyond oneself through the diverse perspectives of its members. We both acknowledged the need for strategic thinkers and visionary individuals within WITI to propel the organization forward.

As we continued, Carolyn shared her passion for WITI and the strategic approach behind its initiatives, emphasizing the profound impact of creating a network of diverse, smart individuals who not only teach directly but also provide indirect insights crucial for personal and professional growth.

I seized the opportunity to share a real-world example of WITI's power in action during a cybersecurity incident at MGM. A consultant, encountered in a WITI session, provided me with a valuable article, which I passed on to the head of cybersecurity at Eversource, my engagement as a consultant, at the time. This ripple effect showcased the tangible benefits of WITI's network in sharing critical knowledge.

Our conversation resonated deeply with the strategic approach behind WITI's initiatives, creating a space where professionals can exchange ideas, knowledge, and experiences to become smarter and better at what they do.

We delved into the essence of WITI, where seemingly small connections during sessions lead to meaningful relationships and opportunities. Carolyn highlighted the importance of not only possessing knowledge but also ensuring that it is known, reinforcing the value of WITI's platform.

Our conversation concluded with Carolyn expressing her overwhelming need to solve the challenges faced by women in tech, leading her to establish WITI. As we wrapped up, Carolyn shared her excitement about the prospect of continuing our engaging discussions over dinner during my next visit to the West Coast.

This journey with Carolyn Leighton has been an enriching experience, unveiling the transformative power of mentorship, the magic of networks, and the importance of embracing uniqueness. As we navigate the ever-evolving landscape of technology, let's carry forward the lessons learned, celebrating diversity, fostering connections, and empowering one another to reach new heights.

Cheers to the magic of WITI, the power of connections, and the endless possibilities in the world of technology!

> "My vision in WITI was rooted in the belief that creating a platform for women with diverse technological expertise could be a game-changer. It struck me that assembling a group of women spanning various professions, from lawyers to scientists and beyond, hailing from different cultural backgrounds, could cultivate a dynamic network. The idea was to provide them with the means to collaborate, especially when faced with challenges that could influence their career trajectory positively—be it securing a promotion or leading a pivotal project. This vision was born from my prior experiences, including my time with a research company where Hewlett Packard (HP) left an indelible mark on my approach.

> In essence, the model I envisioned for WITI was inspired by the authentic diversity I witnessed at Hewlett-Packard. It went beyond the conventional notion of diversity groups, transcending labels, and embraced the true essence of diverse perspectives. This strategy, often overlooked in conversations about diversity and inclusion, became the cornerstone of WITI's blueprint—an organization that empowers women with a spectrum of technological expertise to connect, collaborate, and thrive in the ever-evolving landscape of the tech industry."

> \- Carolyn Leighton, Founded WITI in 1989

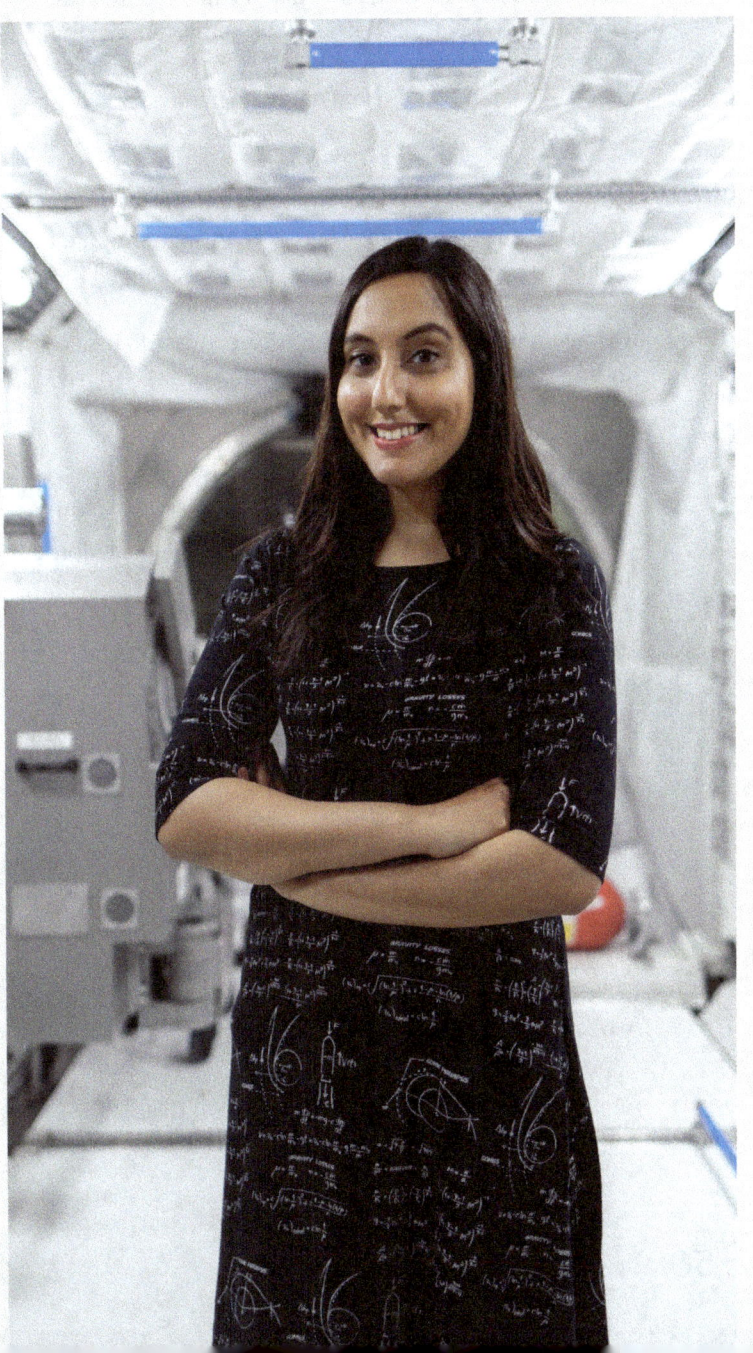

Tips From Tia

Women: How We Can Have It All!

As we celebrate Women's History Month, I think it's important to say that being a woman can be pretty challenging. We have hormonal changes, health changes, and physical changes much more rapidly and sporadic than our other human counterparts. A lot is expected from a woman, as well as things that aren't expected from a woman. Women are expected to be caregivers, nurturing, pretty, soft, put-together, domesticated, sexy, submissive, and the list can go on, …and on. Women have also been NOT expected to rise, conquer, and defeat.

However, with all that said, I find that we are an incredible breed because we are resilient and can shatter that glass ceiling while encompassing and accomplishing all that we really want in this world if we put our minds to it. For a woman today, you can ask her, "Do you want to be a mom, or do you want to be a CEO?" and she will answer "Yes," if that's what she really wants.

I'm sure you are familiar with the quote by Laurel Thatcher Ulrich, "Well-behaved women seldom make history." It's been assumed that the quote came from Marilyn Monroe, but in fact, the quote came out of an article on a Puritan funeral service in 1976. And I'm confident that many incredible women, including Marilyn, inspired such a quote to hold fast. Because, love or hate her, that blonde bombshell broke a lot of glass on her rise by showing other women there are ways to be business savvy while in stilettos.

The point is that women have a fantastic opportunity to be everything they want to be. And for women who want it all, they can get it all. But the truth is, we all need some help and guidance along the way. And that's not because we're women. We need help because we're human, just like a man who needs help and guidance along the way too.

So here are a few tips when it comes to leveling up as a woman while living in a world that's half-full of men.

Never Be Afraid to Ask

No woman wants to be thought of as the stereotypical damsel in distress. Somewhere along the way, society made a foolish assumption that asking for help was a sure sign of weakness. How wrong society was. Today, thanks to AI and search engines, we can ask a device for help and get some decent answers relatively quickly. However, spending time on the wrong things can be a colossal waste of time when you have someone who already knows the answer standing near you.

I'm not going to lie; asking for help is a tightrope walk. After all, you can't become reliant on others to answer your every whim, like your phone, because you could be labeled incompetent. However, when you need guidance, or even better, to know that you're asking the right questions to reach a successful outcome, please don't be too proud to ask for a helping hand.

Know There Is Enough for Us All

One of the most significant flaws many women have is thinking there isn't enough to go around. That is why, for decades, women have put down other women or ended up in squabbles or that stereotypical cat-fighting bashing with one another. This type of behavior could easily be seen, especially in the entertainment world for many years. You see, many women didn't compete with men back in the day because they didn't know they could. Unfortunately, though, they competed with other women over who's better, over men, over appearance, over briskets, and who knows what else. Still, I'm here to say to anyone who hasn't heard this yet: there is plenty to go around. No one can take something away from you that isn't meant to be yours in the first place. And just because someone else is making big money doesn't mean there isn't enough money for you out there in the world. So, get out there and get yours! There is no need to think of anyone else as your competition besides yourself. The largest battle we face every day is ourselves. So get out of your own way and shatter some ceilings.

Oh, and while you're off getting yours, ladies, don't forget to straighten each other's crowns or pull toilet paper off each other's shoes. It's a tough enough world out there to navigate. Let's be kind to each other.

You're Being Hormonal

Have you ever heard this statement, "You're being hormonal"? The truth is, ...you probably are, and there is nothing wrong with that. Hormones are crazy, so it is super important to keep them in balance. Certain foods carry different hormones, so it is essential to eat a well-balanced diet. I recommend asking your OB/GYN to check your hormone levels at least every other year. This is not a routine blood test, so you must ask for it. Knowing your levels can help you understand what you might be lacking or the best things you need to add to your diet. For example, vitamin E is a great source to boost estrogen. Stem cell patches like X39 can help your body activate new stem cells needed to balance your overall system. Talk to your doctor before starting any supplements or changing your dietary habits. Staying balanced is the key to your mental, physical, and emotional health.

Monthly periods can be the enemy for most women. Some days, you might just wish you could wear a blanket around your waist as you motor through your workday. Heavy periods can wreak havoc on your plans for the day, so keep extra essentials on hand or nearby. On heavy days, you should have pads or tampons in your bag or desk. I also recommend a spare pair of pants in the car or in a bag. An overflow can happen in an instant and leave you and your pants feeling red. Please note that if you are going through a pad or tampon in an hour for a few hours, go seek emergency. You shouldn't be losing too much blood too fast.

Bleeding heavily can be associated with many things, including menopause, so make an appointment if you've had changes in your period. Every woman on the planet will inevitably go through the 'CHANGE,' but you can talk with your doctor about going through it gracefully.

Practice Self-Care First

Self-care has finally made it to the center stage after many years of being shunned and labeled selfish or conceited. I give a standing ovation to self-care because we will never achieve being our best selves without it. I have said many times that we must resupply ourselves so we can be kinder to others and that resupplying comes from taking time for ourselves.

Take time to rejuvenate how you know you need to, whether that be a spa day, a fresh haircut, or walking in nature. Taking time to meditate daily can change your mindset and reduce stress. Some women choose to do yoga. Some take a long bath with music and wine. Some ladies that I had talked to decided to get their nails done as their self-care priority. They've told me it's time for them to pamper themselves while getting in 'girl' time and eliminating something that would annoy them if they had to do it on their own. They also felt like it was part of their business wardrobe because it continues to make them feel more confident and put-together.

That's great!

Find things that really fill you to your soul. By resupplying your energy with time and activities that fulfill you on a regular basis, you will find you have much more to give others.

As a woman, you should be able to accomplish all that you want in this world. There are so many inspiring women to look up to who have been able to balance their lives and have everything they want. It would take a million pages to list them all, and it would be too difficult to list a quantifiable handful, so I think it's best to advise you to look in the mirror because it all starts with you.

OMG! Did you hear?

It's never been simpler to employ your people!

 Band of Hands

Introducing our new partnership providing you Turnkey & Stress Free Employment!

At Band of Hands, we make it it simple and cost effective to run your business and employ your beloved staff with our complete employment solution.

How You Benefit

Wave goodbye to the administrative hassles and added costs that come with being an employer.

How Your Staff Benefits

Free up time to create an outstanding culture for your people, while offering health benefits and 401K plans at no cost to you.

GET ALL THE DETAILS AND CONNECT AT:

bandofhands.com/shetalks

Exclusive Offer!!!

She Talks Members – Take $100 off Signup Fee (Regularly $250) and first 30 days of payroll free!

 **Band of Hands**

With Band of Hands as your SINGLE Employment Partner that handles it all, you can relax and just focus on what you love. If it's related to employment, we've got you covered!

Hello, Peace of Mind! Goodbye, Back-office Stress!

We bundle everything in one platform for one low, flat fee of only $12/person per week.

Band of Hands handles all the stuff you don't want to do! Including:

- Your payroll and payroll taxes
- Time & attendance tracking for your staff
- Your HR needs
- Onboarding & offboarding of your staff
- Automated recruiting and job boards for hiring needs

And there's more!

- We help keep you compliant with employment laws.
- We provide FREE paid sick time.
- We process your unemployment and Workers Comp claims.
- We provide your employees health benefits at no cost to you.
- We provide competitive Workers Comp insurance rates.
- Anything you need – just contact us!

GET ALL THE DETAILS AND CONNECT AT:
bandofhands.com/shetalks

Let's chat!

Eve Nasby
eve@bandofhands.com
619.244.3000

Transcending Barriers

By Nuirka Castaneda

March is Women's History Month, a time dedicated to honoring the extraordinary contributions of women across history. In observance of this significant occasion, we pay tribute to exceptional female veterans who have profoundly influenced the U.S. armed forces and society at large. From the Civil War era to the present day, these women have shattered barriers, showcasing unparalleled courage and resilience. Their unwavering dedication to their country has served as an inspiration to over 2.5 million women who have bravely served in the U.S. military. Indeed, their patriotism and courage know no bounds, transcending gender barriers and leaving an enduring legacy for generations to come.

1. Harriet Tubman – Freedom Fighter and Union Spy

She is not only famous for escaping slavery and later rescuing over 70 other slaves as a conductor on the Underground Railroad, but also made significant contributions to the Union during the Civil War. Serving as a cook, nurse, and spy, Tubman played a pivotal role in planning and executing daring military operations. Her bravery and ingenuity saved countless lives and earned her recognition as the first woman to lead a military expedition in American history, resulting in the emancipation of over 750 slaves. Her legacy as a freedom fighter and patriot continues to inspire generations to strive for justice and equality.

Public domain, Wikimedia Commons

2. Sarah Emma Edmonds – Civil War Heroine and Spy

A Canadian by birth, she emigrated to the US leaving an abusive family home under the alias of Franklin Flint Thompson. She enlisted on May 25, 1861 during the Civil War as a disguised Union soldier and spy participating in numerous battles and espionage missions, risking her life to support the Union cause. Her bravery and resourcefulness earned her the admiration of her comrades and secured her place in history as one of the few documented female soldiers of the Civil War.

Kean Collection/Archive Photos/Getty Images

3. Loretta Perfectus Walsh – First Female Enlistee

Following Navy Secretary Josephus Daniels' decision to allow women to join the U.S. Naval Reserve Force to address the challenge of mobilizing forces, she promptly seized the opportunity. On March 21, 1917, only two days later, she enlisted as a Chief Yeoman, heralding a new era of women's contributions to national defense beyond nursing roles. Her historic enlistment garnered extensive national attention and inspired a surge in enlistments, marking a significant milestone in gender equality in the military and recognizing the invaluable contributions of women to the war effort.

US Navy, Public domain, via Wikimedia Commons

4. Colonel Ruby Bradley

United States Army, Public domain, via Wikimedia Commons

A Symbol of Resilience and Fortitude

One of the most decorated women in military history, she endured 37 months as a Japanese prisoner during World War II, earning the title "Angels in Fatigues" alongside fellow imprisoned nurses. Despite enduring unimaginable hardships, she selflessly tended to the wounded, sacrificing her own well-being to alleviate the suffering of others. Bradley's remarkable service, reflected in 34 decorations and medals, embodies the indomitable spirit of the American soldier.

5. Army Gen. Ann E. Dunwoody

United States Army, Public domain, via Wikimedia Commons

Leading with Distinction

She made history as the first woman to achieve the rank of four-star general in the U.S. armed forces. Commissioned as a second lieutenant in the Women's Army Corps in 1975, Dunwoody's illustrious career spanned over three decades, culminating in her role as commander of the Army Materiel Command. Under her leadership, the AMC revolutionized global logistics, ensuring that the joint force remained ready and supplied. Dunwoody's trailblazing career paved the way for future generations of women in the military, demonstrating excellence and leadership at the highest levels.

6. Army: Sgt. Leigh Ann Hester

English: Sergeant Gina Vaile, United States Army, Public domain, via Wikimedia Commons

A Trailblazer in Combat

She made history as the first woman to receive the Silver Star for her courageous actions in Iraq. Leading a counterattack against insurgents who ambushed her convoy, Hester displayed exceptional bravery under fire. Despite facing heavy machine-gun fire and mortar attacks, she fearlessly engaged the enemy. Her actions resulted in 27 insurgents killed, six wounded, one captured and every member of her unit surviving. Hester's valor and leadership epitomize the resilience and dedication of women in combat.

> *"I am a woman and a warrior. If you think I can't be both, you've been lied to."*
>
> — *Jennifer Zeynab Joukhadar*

7. Air Force Col. Merryl Tengesdal
Soaring to New Heights

English: Sergeant Gina Vaile, United States Army, Public domain, via Wikimedia Commons

She defied expectations by becoming the first Black woman to fly the U-2 Dragon Lady spy plane in the Air Force. Transitioning from the Navy to the Air Force, Tengesdal's remarkable career exemplifies courage and perseverance. Flying missions in some of the world's most challenging environments, including Afghanistan and Iraq, she logged over 3,400 flight hours and 330 combat hours. Tengesdal's achievements highlight the importance of diversity and representation in military aviation.

8. Col. Eileen Collins
Reaching for the Stars

By Robert Markowitz - Great Images in NASA (archive) Description (archive), Public Domain, https://commons.wikimedia.org/w/index.php?curid=6449908

Her lifelong passion for aviation propelled her to become the first woman to command a space shuttle mission. Joining the Air Force in 1979, Collins's exemplary career as a pilot and astronaut broke barriers and inspired generations of aspiring astronauts. Her historic command of Space Shuttle mission STS-93 in 1999 marked a milestone in space exploration and solidified her place in history as a pioneering figure in aerospace. Collins's achievements exemplify courage, determination, and the boundless potential of women in STEM fields.

9. Coast Guard: Sara Faulkner
Courage in the Face of Adversity

By U.S. Coast Guard Great Lakes

Sara Faulkner made history as the first female Coast Guard rescue swimmer, demonstrating unparalleled courage and skill in saving lives during Hurricane Katrina saving 48 lives in one night alongside her team. Faulkner's legacy serves as a reminder of the importance of supporting and empowering women in the military.

10. Bea Arthur
Breaking Ground in the Marine Corps

By TV studio - ebay, Public Domain, https://commons.wikimedia.org/w/index.php?curid=29049603

An Emmy & Tony Award-winning actress, best known for her iconic roles in "Maude" and "The Golden Girls," who also made her mark as a trailblazer in the Marine Corps during World War II. Enlisting at the age of 21, under her original name, Bernice Frankel, Arthur became one of the first members of the Women's Reserve. Serving as a truck driver and typist, she rose through the ranks to become a staff sergeant before her honorable discharge in 1945. Arthur's military service laid the foundation for her legendary career in entertainment, where she became a beloved figure and a celebrated advocate for veterans.

••••••••••••••••••••••••••••

As we honor Women's History Month, let us pay tribute to these courageous women who have paved the way for future generations. Their sacrifices, bravery, and unwavering dedication to duty embody the spirit of service and inspire us all to strive for excellence in every endeavor.

THE INCREDIBLE Female CEO

by Shelby Jo Long

Being a leader is challenging in many ways. Stepping into a leadership role is taking on the responsibility of influence and advocacy. In the realm of business leadership, the rise of female CEOs and founders has sparked a profound shift in organizational dynamics. As they ascend to the helm of companies across industries, women bring with them a unique leadership style that challenges traditional norms and transforms workplace cultures. In this article, we explore the distinctive attributes of female leadership and how it can reshape the fabric of organizations.

Historically underrepresented in executive roles, women in leadership positions often approach their roles with a blend of empathy, collaboration, and resilience. Unlike the stereotypical command-and-control model, female CEOs and founders prioritize inclusive decision-making processes and foster environments where diverse voices are heard and valued.

One hallmark of female leadership is the emphasis on emotional intelligence. Studies have shown that women tend to excel in interpersonal skills, empathy, and intuition, traits that are invaluable in navigating complex organizational dynamics. By cultivating a culture of empathy and understanding, female leaders create workplaces where employees feel supported, respected, and empowered to thrive.

Moreover, female CEOs and founders often champion a collaborative leadership style. Rather than relying solely on top-down directives, they engage employees at all levels in problem-solving and decision-making. By soliciting input from diverse perspectives, these leaders harness the collective intelligence of their teams and drive innovation from within.

Another key aspect of female leadership is resilience in the face of adversity. Many women CEOs and founders have overcome formidable obstacles on their journey to the top, whether it's breaking through glass ceilings, balancing work and family responsibilities, or navigating systemic bias. This resilience not only inspires confidence among employees but also fosters a culture of perseverance and grit within the organization.

Female leaders are adept at fostering a culture of mentorship and support. Recognizing the importance of representation and mentorship in advancing women's careers, they actively mentor and sponsor aspiring leaders within their organizations. By nurturing talent and providing opportunities for growth, they create a pipeline of future leaders who reflect the diversity of their workforce.

In addition to these individual leadership attributes, female CEOs and founders often prioritize diversity, equity, and inclusion (DEI) initiatives within their organizations. Recognizing the business imperative of diversity, they champion policies and practices that promote fairness, equality, and belonging. By fostering a culture of inclusion, they not only attract top talent but also drive innovation and creativity through diverse perspectives.

One of the most significant ways in which female CEOs and founders transform organizational culture is by challenging traditional power structures and fostering a more equitable workplace. By dismantling hierarchical barriers and promoting a culture of transparency and accountability, they create environments where meritocracy thrives, and everyone has an opportunity to succeed.

Moreover, female leaders are often more attuned to the needs and priorities of diverse stakeholders, including employees, customers, and communities. By aligning business objectives with social responsibility and sustainability goals, they demonstrate a commitment to creating shared value for all stakeholders, not just shareholders.

In conclusion, the leadership style of female CEOs and founders is a powerful force for driving organizational change and fostering inclusive cultures. By prioritizing empathy, collaboration, resilience, and diversity, these leaders create workplaces where everyone can thrive and contribute their fullest potential. As more women ascend to leadership positions, their transformative influence will continue to reshape the landscape of business and society for the better.

FLORENCE HALL
A Pioneer in the Medical Field

By Terrilani Chong

Florence Hall was born on August 17, 1923, in Brooklyn New York, the second child and eldest daughter of George and Marjorie Hall. During her childhood, Florence knew early on that she would become a nurse.

When she was about 7, a friend of hers was injured in an accident of some sort, and when the ambulance came to take him to the hospital, she insisted she be allowed to ride along. She was not allowed to do so, but that didn't stop her – she ran along behind it for as long as she could.

Florence and her mother Marjorie, circa 1945.

Later, when Florence and her brother Ruddy were maybe 13 and 16 respectively, Ruddy's big toe had become badly infected and one day Florence saw it. The doctor was summoned to the house and he had to drain the toe. Florence assisted him and he was so impressed by her natural skill that he praised her and encouraged her to pursue a nursing career.

She was educated in the public school system of New York, graduating from Erasmus High School, and went on to enroll in King's County Hospital Center School of Nursing, graduating from that establishment in 1944.

Because WWII was happening, and many of the doctors and nurses were in armed service at the time, the student nurses at King's County got to perform services that they would otherwise have only watched. In fact, she was a member of the first human trials team for penicillin – administering the drug to patients to test its efficacy.

It was during her enrollment at King's County that she met the love of her life, James Lee "Buzz" Busby, a member of the United States Coast Guard at the time.

The early days of marriage were tough on the young couple. Flo was required to be in residence at the dorms at King's County, and in fact was forbidden to marry during her training. So, she would sneak out of the dorm at night, with her bed linens, and spend the evening and most of the night with her new husband, before then sneaking back in again. Her marital status was quickly revealed when she conceived her first child, Barbara, known to her family as Boni.

Flo's pregnancy was difficult, and she was required to take a leave of absence in order to have Boni. She subsequently returned to her training, but had to put Boni in the care of her neighbors during the week. As heartbreaking as that was for her to do, her passion for the field of nursing was strong enough to compel her to do this. She and Boni had matching uniforms, with Boni's made lovingly by Flo.

Once she completed her RN and passed her state board exams, Flo devoted herself to raising her children – Boni was followed three years later by James, known to his family as Rusty because of his bright red hair, which he inherited from Flo's mother, Marjorie. A long hiatus ensued before Terrilani was born eight years after Rusty's appearance.

The family moved around often due to Buzz's career in the Coast Guard. They spent a few years in the New York area, where Buzz was a member of the crew of a ship that captured a German submarine that was actually in the New York harbor. From New York, they relocated to New Jersey.

The real traveling began when the family was transferred to Hawaii in 1950. Buzz went out ahead of time and secured housing, while Flo and her sister Irene drove across the country with Boni and Rusty in the back seat of the car. Flo had gotten her driver's license for the express purpose of driving to California and boarding a ship to meet Buzz in Hawaii. Imagine your first real drive being a 3,000 mile jaunt – with two small children along for the ride!

They spent five years in Hawaii, with Terrilani arriving at the end of that period. From Hawaii, they went to Miami for three years, followed by a move to San Juan, Puerto Rico for another three year stay. After San Juan, the family moved to Morehead City in North Carolina again for three years, and from there went to the New London area of Connecticut.

Two generations of nurses: Florence and her daughter Boni (as a baby and later as a graduate of KCHC).

The Busby Family: James L. – aka Buzz, Florence, Barbara – aka Boni, James R. – aka Rusty, and Terrilani.

It was there that Buzz retired from the Coast Guard after a career of building lighthouses and Long Range Navigation (LORAN) stations, and rebuilding storm stricken areas at his various duty stations.

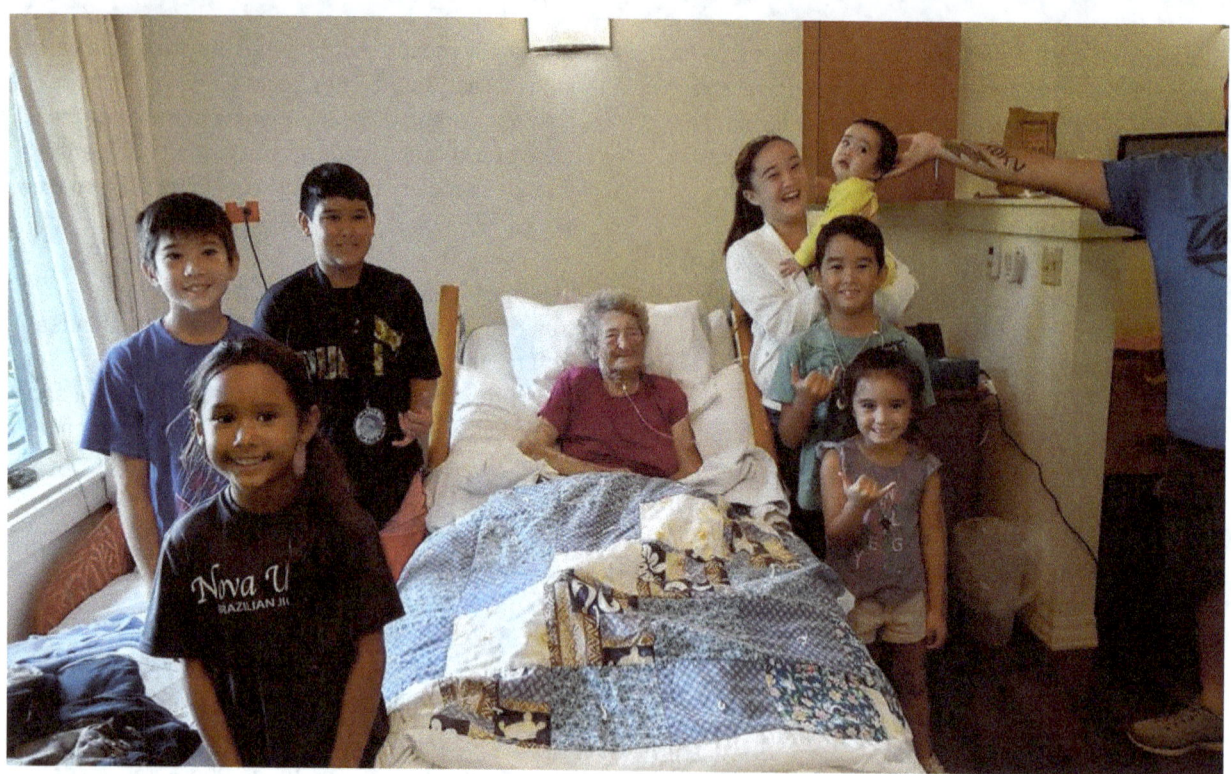

During their time in Connecticut, Flo finally began to pursue her passion, beginning her nursing career as an IV therapist and the person who took the EKGs in the hospital – more than 20 years after graduating as a Registered Nurse from King's County. She quickly progressed to patient care, her true calling, and identified a need for critical care at the small local hospital where she worked. She suggested to two of the doctors she worked with that having an Intensive Care Unit would be a boon to patient care at the hospital, and the board told them to go ahead and design one.

So, she did! The hospital opened its first ICU in 1966, which Florence became Head Nurse of. That unit created a sea change in the culture of Backus Hospital, and as the hospital expanded its campus and care capabilities, a second unit was designed and headed by Florence. She went on to design the third Critical Care Unit just prior to her retirement in 1988, and it was named for her. Quite an honor for an RN!

Florence ushered in a strong tradition of nursing in her family: her younger sister Alice and her children Boni and Rusty went on to be accomplished nurses, while two nieces Gwenn and Debbie and great-nephew Andrew have also entered the profession. When Andrew graduated from nursing school, he asked for a kukui nut lei that Florence had worn on her 92nd birthday. He said he wanted some of Florence's mana (spiritual power) to help him as he started out in nursing. He was eager to let Florence know that he went into critical care nursing just as she did. It is clear to all the family that Florence was someone to emulate.

THE FLORENCE H. BUSBY CRITICAL CARE UNIT

IN HONOR OF
FLORENCE H. BUSBY, R.N.

FOR HER VISION
AND COMMITMENT TO THE ART OF
CRITICAL CARE NURSING

Andrew Durham with his kukui nut lei.

Florence's love of nursing is also reflected in a comment she made after she chose to enter hospice.

"Now I have experienced every aspect of nursing."

True to form, she spoke encouragingly to her care givers there, just as she had done in any medical setting, offering them kind words and telling them how important their career choices were.

Florence eventually relocated to Hawaii permanently and lived out her final years as a member of the Honomu community, celebrating her 95th and final birthday in August of 2018. Her friends and family surrounded her during her final months as she slowed down ever so slightly, but overall her health was in very good trim until her final couple of weeks when kidney failure overtook her. She spent her last days at Hospice of Hilo, where she was comfortable and well cared for by their staff and visited by many of her friends and family. She was never alone during this time, and passed with family at her side – eager to rejoin her "partner, that man with the most beautiful smile."

Aloha Florence! You were a woman of fierce dedication to your family, your career, and your world.

Florence and Buzz – "that man with the most beautiful smile" – enjoying their final dance circa 1982.

From Fort Living Room to Fort Knox

Beatrice's Journey of Adversity and Triumph

by Wendy Watson

BEATRICE BRUNO

In the bustling streets of New York City, Beatrice's journey began in the tumultuous backdrop of family turmoil and societal prejudices. Born in 1959, her early life was marked by the complexities of familial discord and racial discrimination. Separated from her biological parents at a tender age, she was raised by her grandparents in the heart of South Carolina, unaware of her true lineage until her teenage years. "I had no idea my oldest brother was my dad."

Growing up in the racially charged atmosphere of the 1960s and 70s, Beatrice confronted the harsh reality of being a dark-skinned black girl in a society that often devalued her worth based on the color of her skin. "I was always told as a little black girl, that I was too black to be pretty, too black to be anything in life, too black to be successful." Taunted with derogatory slurs and subjected to systemic discrimination, she encountered adversity at every turn. Yet, fueled by a fiery determination to defy the odds, Beatrice found solace in the promise of a better future, one that beckoned her beyond the confines of her hometown.

Her decision to join the Army was not merely a leap into the unknown but a defiant stance against those who doubted her capabilities. "I was standing there looking at the sign that read, "Be all you can be. US Army needs you". And I looked at the sign. And this big, tall white guy in the army uniform came out. He said, "young lady, can I help you?" And I said, "Well, yes, sir, would the Army take someone like me?" And he said, "What's wrong with you?" I said, "well, I got a kid & I'm black. I don't know. Would the army take me?" He said: "Of course the Army would take you." and that did it for me." Motivated by a desire to escape the limitations imposed upon her and inspired by her uncle's skepticism about women in the military, Beatrice embarked on a journey of self-discovery and resilience. Little did she know that this decision would transform her life in ways she could never have imagined.

Marching into Fort Jackson, South Carolina, for basic training in 1977, Beatrice embraced the rigorous challenges of military life with unwavering determination. Despite the lingering shadows of racism and sexism that pervaded the armed forces, she refused to be confined by societal expectations or prejudiced ideologies. As she recalls, "I never looked back."

Throughout her 15-year tenure in the Army, Beatrice confronted numerous obstacles, both on and off the battlefield. From navigating the treacherous terrain of racial tensions in the Deep South to confronting the insidious specter of sexual assault within the ranks, she grappled with adversity at every turn. Yet, through sheer grit and tenacity, she emerged as a beacon of resilience, defying the odds and shattering glass ceilings along the way.

It was during her time as a drill sergeant that Beatrice found her true calling. Tasked with molding raw recruits into disciplined soldiers, she reveled in the opportunity to impart wisdom and instill confidence in the next generation. For Beatrice, being a drill sergeant was more than just a duty; it was a privilege — a chance to empower others and shape the course of their lives. "So one of my soldiers that graduated from basic training in 1988. Under me. He is a a movie producer now. He produces movies and he stars in some of these movies and stuff. Yes, A couple of the soldiers became sergeant's major. And you know, and I'm just so proud of all of them because they made something of their lives."

Reflecting on her transformative journey from Fort Living Room to Fort Knox, Beatrice exudes a sense of pride and accomplishment. Her mantra, "I'm gonna get mine," serves as a testament to her indomitable spirit and unwavering resolve. Through perseverance and perseverance alone, Beatrice Bruno, The Drill Sergeant of Life defied the odds, transcended adversity, and carved out her own path to success.

"I was just a measly E. 5, sergeant. but I had the persona and the character of the sergeant first class."

As the Drill Sergeant of Life, Beatrice Bruno drills "It's all in how you project yourself & to take ownership of what you want."

As she imparts her wisdom to others, Beatrice embodies the epitome of resilience — a testament to the power of the human spirit to triumph over adversity and adversity. From the dusty streets of South Carolina to the hallowed halls of military excellence to embodying "The Drill Sergeant of Life", her journey serves as an inspiration to all who dare to dream and defy the odds. Beatrice's story is a reminder that, in the face of adversity, the human spirit is capable of achieving the extraordinary.

Wendy Watson
Spiritual Therapist, Speaker, Author
TBR Spiritual Health
720-782-6090
Wendy@tbrspiritualhealth.com
Tbrspiritualhealth.com

SYNERGY LEARNING

INSTITUTE

ACCREDITED COURSES
501(C)(3)

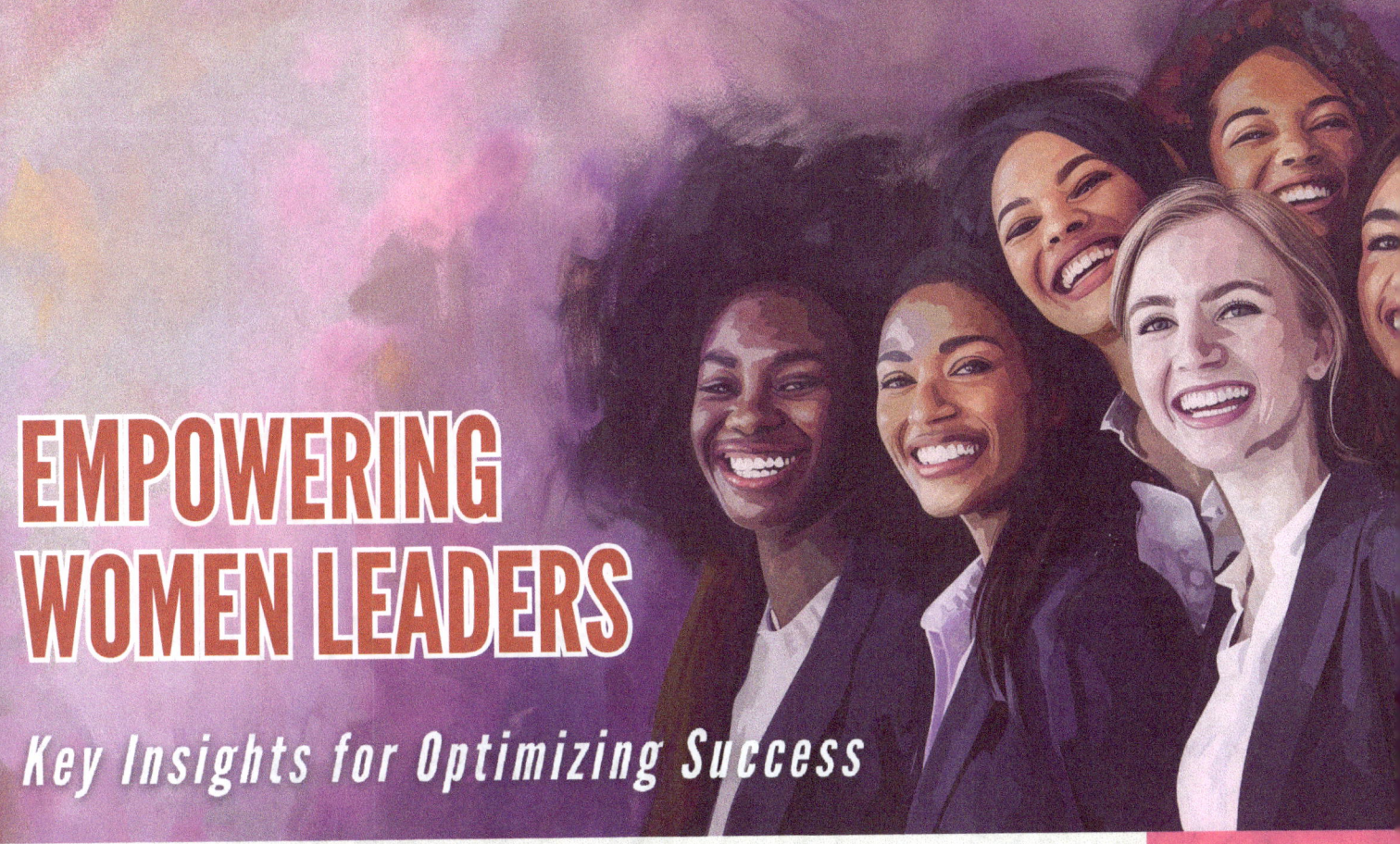

EMPOWERING WOMEN LEADERS

Key Insights for Optimizing Success

by Kim-adele Randall

In today's dynamic and ever-evolving professional landscape, women leaders are making significant strides, breaking barriers, and reshaping industries. Yet, despite advancements, challenges persist, necessitating a nuanced understanding of what women leaders need to optimize their success. Empowerment, resilience, and strategic acumen are crucial pillars for women leaders to build their path to success. Here are some insightful, actionable, and knowledgeable strategies for women leaders to navigate and thrive in their leadership journey.

1. Embrace Authentic Leadership

Authenticity lies at the heart of effective leadership. Women leaders must embrace their unique strengths, values, and perspectives, leveraging them to inspire and motivate others. Authenticity fosters trust, enhances credibility, and cultivates genuine connections with team members, fostering a culture of openness and collaboration.

2. Cultivate Resilience

Resilience is a cornerstone of success in leadership roles. Women leaders must anticipate and navigate obstacles with grace and determination. Embracing setbacks such as learning opportunities, maintaining a positive mindset, and developing adaptive coping strategies are essential for resilience. By bouncing back from adversity, women leaders demonstrate their strength and inspire those around them to persevere in the face of challenges.

3. Prioritize Self-Care

Amidst the demands of leadership, prioritizing self-care is paramount. Women leaders must recognize the importance of maintaining physical, mental, and emotional well-being. Establishing boundaries, practicing mindfulness, and incorporating regular exercise and adequate rest into their routines are essential for sustaining high performance and preventing burnout.

4. Foster Inclusive Leadership

Inclusive leadership is indispensable for fostering innovation, driving productivity, and nurturing a diverse and equitable workplace. Women leaders should actively champion diversity, equity, and inclusion initiatives, creating opportunities for underrepresented voices to be heard and valued. By fostering an inclusive culture, women leaders cultivate environments where individuals feel empowered to contribute their unique perspectives and talents.

5. Continuously Develop Skills

The journey to leadership excellence is a continuous learning process. Women leaders must invest in their personal and professional development, acquiring new skills and knowledge to stay ahead in a rapidly evolving landscape. Seeking out mentors, participating in leadership development programs, and pursuing ongoing education are valuable strategies for honing leadership capabilities and staying competitive in the marketplace.

6. Build Strong Networks

Networking is instrumental in advancing careers and accessing new opportunities. Women leaders should actively cultivate diverse networks within and outside their organizations. Building strong relationships with peers, mentors, and industry leaders provides valuable support and guidance and opens doors to collaborations, partnerships, and career advancement prospects.

7. Advocate for Yourself

Self-advocacy is critical for women leaders to advance their careers and attain the recognition they deserve. Women leaders must confidently articulate their achievements, skills, and aspirations, advocating for themselves in negotiations, performance evaluations, and career advancement discussions. By owning their worth and communicating their value proposition, women leaders can position themselves for success and overcome systemic barriers.

8. Lead with Empathy

Empathy is a powerful leadership trait that fosters trust, enhances communication, and strengthens relationships. Women leaders should cultivate empathy by actively listening to the needs and concerns of their team members, demonstrating understanding, and offering support and encouragement. By leading empathetically, women leaders create inclusive and supportive environments where individuals feel valued, respected, and empowered to thrive.

As women continue to ascend to leadership positions across industries, equipping themselves with the insights, skills, and strategies outlined above is crucial for optimizing their success. By embracing authenticity, resilience, self-care, inclusive leadership, continuous learning, networking, self-advocacy, and empathy, women leaders can navigate challenges, seize opportunities, and make lasting contributions to their organizations and beyond. Empowered women leaders inspire others and pave the way for a more inclusive and equitable future.

CONNECT WITH KIM

https://www.facebook.com/authenticachievements

https://www.instagram.com/kimadele10/

https://www.linkedin.com/in/kimadele/

https://www.youtube.com/c/AuthenticAchievements

Cultivating Gratitude in Challenging Times: *A Guide for Resilience*

By *Shannon Missimer*

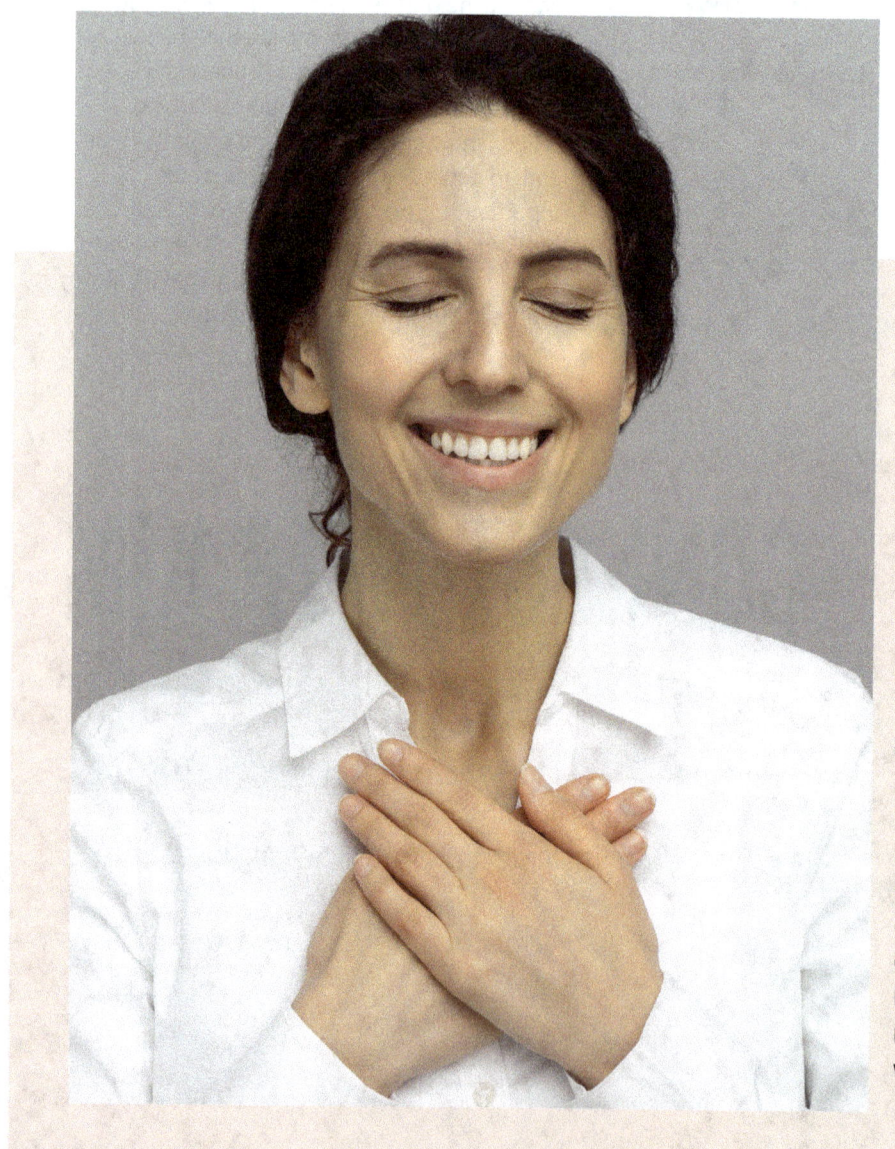

In the intensity of life's challenges, it's something that can be so overlooked, yet often gratitude acts as our steady anchor, bringing us back into the present to truly experience the beauty of life. As we celebrate Women's History Month, it's a beautiful reminder to reflect on the resilience of women who have faced adversity with grace and gratitude, paving the way for generations to come. Here, we will explore practical strategies to cultivate gratitude amidst challenging times, drawing inspiration from the resilience of remarkable women throughout history.

The Power of Gratitude to Illuminate Even the Darkest Moments"

When we enter a season where life gets rough, it's easy to lose sight of the blessings in the chaos. Yet, it's precisely during these turbulent moments that a gratitude practice becomes so powerful. Consider the story of Maya Angelou, she once said, "This is a wonderful day. I've never seen this one before." Even in the darkest of times, Angelou found solace in the simple beauty of a new day, a sentiment that speaks volumes about the power of gratitude to uplift us, no matter the circumstances. And even in our own day to day lives, when we can't always pull inspiration from the heroic stories of others, in our own dark moments; in the trenches of motherhood with little babies, in our professional lives juggling deadlines, frustrated customers and coworkers, and dreams that feel so out of reach some days, the practice of gratitude takes us out of the thought of What IF and brings us deeply into the knowing of What IS.

Cultivating Gratitude When Faced with Adversity

So, how can we cultivate gratitude when faced with adversity? One approach is to start small but consistent. Begin each day by reflecting on three things you're grateful for, allow yourself to sit in thoughts and feelings that would otherwise pass us by. Whether it's that first sip of a cup of coffee or the fact that you have a moment of quiet before entering the fast pace of the day. By grounding ourselves in these moments of appreciation, we train our minds to reach for the positives, even in the midst of intensity. Not only are we thinking about the positive, practicing gratitude has been linked to improved physical health. Studies have shown that individuals who engage in gratitude practices exhibit lower blood pressure, reduced inflammation, and improved cardiovascular health. It appears that the act of acknowledging and appreciating the positive aspects of life can have a direct impact not only on our mental well-being but also, on our physiological well-being.

The Power to Reframe

Another powerful tool for cultivating gratitude is the practice of reframing challenges as opportunities for growth. Take the story of Malala Yousafzai, who, despite facing unimaginable adversity, found gratitude in her ability to advocate for girls' education worldwide. By shifting our perspective from victimhood to empowerment, we can uncover hidden blessings amidst the chaos, building our resilience in the process. Something like this can feel so small, yet again the powerful impact of intentionally reframing is the catalyst to true shifts in the way we see the world.

Find Your People

In addition to personal reflection, community support can play a pivotal role in nurturing gratitude during difficult times. Sometimes one of the most powerful things we can do is reach out to friends, family, or someone who can offer encouragement and solidarity on your journey. Share stories of gratitude and resilience, and honestly just a space where you can acknowledge one another and feel less alone in the daily grind that we can all sometimes get lost in.

During Women's History Month, let us draw inspiration from the countless women who have taken the road less traveled (or never traveled!), yet emerged stronger and more resilient than ever. From Rosa Parks to Ruth Bader Ginsburg, their legacies remind us of the transformative power of gratitude in the face of adversity. As we honor their contributions, let us also commit to nurturing our own resilience through intentional gratitude, knowing that even in the darkest of times, there is always something to be grateful for.

It's more than a nice idea- It's a Powerful Tool

Cultivating gratitude in challenging times is not merely a lofty ideal but a practical tool for resilience and empowerment. By embracing a gratitude practice rooted in mindfulness, reframing challenges as opportunities, and seeking support from our communities, we can weather life's storms with grace and resilience. As we celebrate Women's History Month, let us honor the resilience of women past and present by cultivating gratitude in our own lives, knowing that through gratitude, we can find strength in even the most challenging of times.

https://www.facebook.com/shannon.missimer/
https://www.instagram.com/shannonmissimer/
https://www.linkedin.com/in/shannonmissimer/
https://www.youtube.com/@themotionofgratitude

Connect with Shannon

by Heather Coe Clark

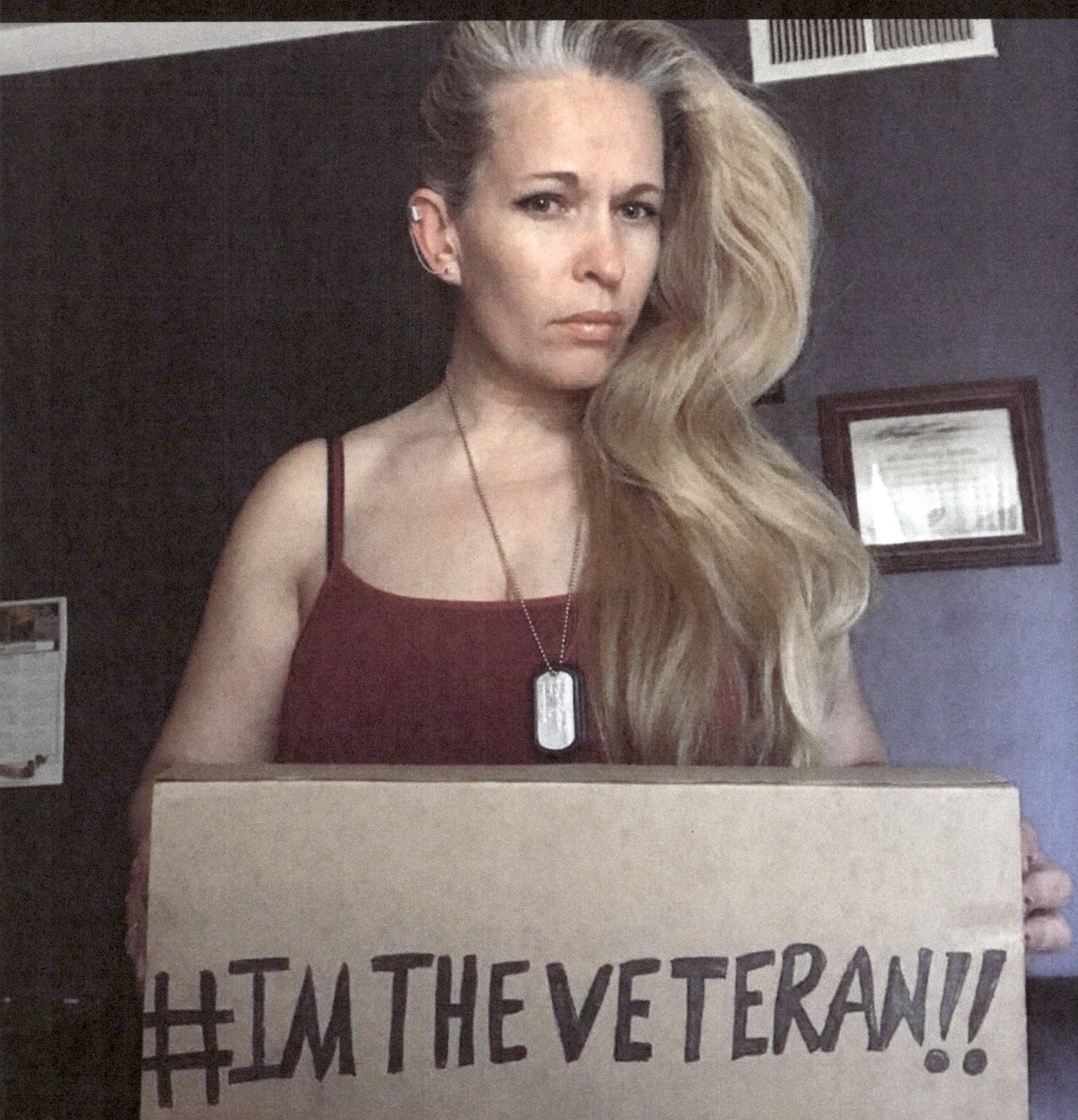

"Excuse me Mam, that parking space is for veterans. Yes, I know, I am a veteran. No mam if your husband is with you, you can park there, but otherwise you need to park in another space."

From being confronted about parking in a veteran space to a male dominated healthcare, business and nonprofit world, female veterans are often overlooked, dismissed and not a part of the American military story.

Hello, my name is Heather Coe Clark and I Am The Veteran.

Throughout history women have been a part of the centuries old movement called war. Conflicts that arose around the world where an opposing group responded with an armed engagement to defend territory and freedom. From tending to the wounded, to putting on the uniform in secret to the women today that serve in every branch of the military. Women have always been part of the movement to defend liberty and freedom and vital to the continuation of America.

The modern female veteran may be allowed to join the military, wear the uniform, and receive services, but the number of resources available compared to male counterparts is anything but equal. Recognition of their contributions and consideration of their needs are often an afterthought and only considered if proactively pushed by a female veteran. The Post 9/11 generation is dominated with male veteran stories of courage and sacrifice, flooded with male veteran podcasts, books, movies and nonprofits.

An absence of women's place in military history is the most glaring in American cinema. The modern-day storyteller of our culture and history, influences the collective mindset of who is and isn't significant in the mission to defend our country. Military movies are often the most memorable filled with action and stories of courage, bravery, and brotherhood. What about the sisters? There are a handful of movies that have included women in the military and have not received the recognition or accolades of males' stories. Even the actresses that have played in this handful of productions have seen the lack of recognition and value in telling our stories.

Demi Moore, one of the most well-known actresses in the world has played in two military movies as both a supporting and main lead character. In her book "Inside Out" she talks about how directors did not see the need to keep her in, A Few Good Men because there was no romantic relationship between her and the main character. One director stated "Why didn't we just cast a male, if there isn't going to be any sexual relationship with the other officer?" He saw no need for a female military officer in the film if there was no sex involved.

In GI Jane she played the main character that told the story of a woman who made it through the most grueling of all military trainings to become an elite part of the US Navy Seals. Demi was disappointed to see that all the hard work she put in mentally and physically to tell the story of a female in the military would be considered as just a novelty film with no real impact.

Recognition of any group that directly contributes to a movement or action that impacts an entire country is deserving of the same respect and accolades of their counterparts. Recognition is the key to unlocking the door to other struggles that female veterans face, from that veteran parking space to equal resources after we get out. Once female veterans are truly recognized for their input, value, and place in that military story then the collective mindset will follow. So, let's start there, thank you sisters, for your resilience, for your strength, courage and for your unwavering patriotism to defend and serve our great nation. They couldn't have done it without you.

Hollywood if your listening, call me.

Sincerely Yours,
Heather Coe Clark
The Veteran

https://www.instagram.com/i_am_the_veteran/

https://www.linkedin.com/in/heather-coe-clark-mph-us-navy-veteran-484545110/

EMPOWERING WOMEN IN BUSINESS TO UNLEASH THEIR AUTHENTIC GENIUS

Program is 🔥

Results and ROI! These ladies and their team are the real deal.

AUTHENTIC GENIUS PROGRAM

WHAT'S INCLUDED

- Monthly Business Coaching
- Authentic Genius Book
- Authentic Genius Magazine Feature
- TEDx Training & Signature Keynote
- Book Signing
- Branding and Marketing
- PR Positioning

✉ JULIEMDUCHARME@GMAIL.COM

✉ SHELBY@BUSINESSDYNAMICS.AGENCY

YOURAUTHENTICGENIUS.COM

ABOUT THE PROGRAM

Your Authentic Genius is a groundbreaking *12-month program* led by Dr. Julie Ducharme and Shelby Jo Long. This unique program is designed exclusively for female business leaders, aiming to propel them to the next level in their professional and personal journeys. The program offers a comprehensive approach that covers business and leadership coaching, branding, scaling, book authorship, keynote speaking, and public engagement.

LEAD AND EMPOWER HER
She —TALKS—
MEMBERSHIP

Join the movement
Only $60/yr

- B2B Networking (30k connections)
- Conferences and Speaking Opportunities
- Magazine Spotlights
- Private App

and much more

Join Today @ shetalks.locals.com

and get a She Talks Hat